APERTURE

D1608402

PEDRO MEYER, The Lady and Her Servants, Mexico, 1979

Latin American Photography

"History is a prophet who looks back, and because of what is and against what was, announces what will be," said Eduardo Galeano, Uruguayan-born writer. This selection of photography from Latin America reveals at once a great emotional power yoked to intellectual passion, and a grasp of historicity. It reveals the sense of the magnitude of a heritage: Spanish, black and Indian, each strain equally complex.

The differences between the many peoples of Latin America visible in these images are imposed by geography, blood and class, and exacerbated by a legacy of poverty, oppression, and social injustice. Even their myths are brutally real: stories of conquest, of servitude, of lost language and lost gods. The dialogue with past and future time "emerges from the mysteries of a land which seems to demand suffering to grow and succeed," said the poet Fernando Alegria.

A fierce sense of ideology exists, the result of the corrosive effect of fear and injustice on the social fabric. From conquistadores to technocrats, from the dividends of the slave trade to the profits of United Brands, every country has undergone its own dark cycles of repressive dictatorships, and foreign interventions. Dark, too, is their syncretic religion with its dead and resurrected hopes, its fertile sacrifices. These undercurrents provide a clue to how many Latin Americans see their politics: a hybrid of indigenous struggle and international domination.

What the Latin American photographers represented seem to share, then, is a belief that art should be at the service of a social change. And as culture is a process of negotiation, so the visual images here are hard-won concessions on the photographers' own terms. The questions they raise point out the difficulty of formulating a language for the special circumstances, challenges, and dreams of a continent in the process of seismic change. This issue attempts to communicate recognition of their vital debate, which is producing work of such concentration and sympathy that we can only ask to see more.

This issue began with the vision and guidance of Fred Ritchin, who curated the exhibition of Contemporary Latin American photographers seen at the Burden Gallery this year. The exhibition, touring under the auspices of Aperture, provided many of the images for this publication.

THE EDITORS

Six Stations of the Latino American Via Crucis

By Edmundo Desnoes

Latino America is a hum in the background, a hum that once in a blue moon becomes a strident scream. But whatever the stereophonic level, Latino America remains unintelligible for most Anglo Americans.

The clash in the New World began more than two hundred years ago. It all started with the defeat of the "Armada Invencible" in 1588, which marked the defeat of Latino passion by Anglo pragmatism. "The Spaniards and the Anglo Americans are, properly speaking, the two races that divide the possession of the New World," said Alexis de Tocqueville, a third party of sorts, in 1835, when he foretold the outcome of the struggle for possession of the continent: "The limits of separation between them have been settled by treaty; but although the conditions of that treaty are favorable to the Anglo Americans, I do not doubt that they will shortly infringe it."

Southern voices were briefly audible in the U. S.: during the Mexican Revolution when John Reed and Sergei Eisenstein went to cover the struggle; when General Pershing entered Mexico to punish Pancho Villa. But it all came to an end when Diego Rivera had the gall to include Lenin in his Rockefeller Center mural. Nelson Rockefeller then ordered every inch, every chip of the mural removed and crushed. A few decades later another strident Latino scream heralded the Cuban Revolution. Fidel Castro made the covers of *Time* and *Life* and *Newsweek*, more than once. And Che Guevara became a cult hero for dissatisfied middle-class students, an anomaly which ended when student leaders rejoined mainstream America. One kind of Latino import lasted longer: the tango, the bolero, the conga, the rhumba, the mambo and the samba which flavored Anglo American music for over fifty years. But today, Latino sound has lost much of its original big band form and significance.

One of the most surprising elements of this dispute within the body of the continent is how boisterously the battle has taken place in the South, and how soundlessly it has developed in the North.

The Latino world still occupies half of the continent, even though this fact becomes obscured by the shift of U.S. interests—both economic and cultural—toward the nations of the Pacific. We have not disappeared. On the contrary, Central America has become an irritant: the frontier with Mexico is 1,933 miles of instability, and twenty million Latinos inhabit the shadows of the Southwest and the Atlantic and Pacific coasts of the United States.

Why do so many people appear to mean so little for most Anglo Americans? If we put aside for a moment the threat of Communism and the appeal of Inca, Maya and Aztec arts and crafts, maybe we can try and break the barrier of too much noise or too much silence.

Latino American photography can, perhaps, give us an oblique entrance where the volumes of history, the anthropological studies, and the baroque literature certainly haven't helped much. Within the photography included in the following pages, the photographers have given us the visual signs of a code. The code is opaque, the signs are illegible, yet these are "photos à clef," allowing us to make six stops in the via crucis of Latino American imagery. Other possible stations are of limited regional importance, whether historical or structural. These universal stations are understood both inside and outside the region: Revolution, Love, Religion, U.S. Penetration, Nature, and Children.

Station I: Revolution Let us begin with the Mexican Revolution of 1910. A new awareness usually follows a threat, a basic change, a shift in power. And the Mexican Revolution represented all of these. Marking for the world the appearance of the sombrero, the loose white peasant garment, guaraches, and the revolutionary rifle, the Mexican Revolution created an identity of the hero that extended almost down to Patagonia. Pancho Villa began to inhabit the imagination of the Anglo American. On the screen, Wallace Beery became Pancho Villa and rode into the active role of Latino imagery, to be enriched in the early fifties by Marlon Brando who became Emiliano Zapata in an Elia Kazan film.

Reports of the revolution spread from Emiliano Zapata, Pancho Villa, and the people of Mexico to Latino America through photos, news items and film—then to Anglo America, Europe, Africa and Asia—and then back to Latino America. Latino American photographers are conditioned by visual codes, but these codes were often established abroad. The photographers in Mexico, Cuba, Argentina or Nicaragua, for example, see social upheaval from a vantage point of historical experience, focusing on the physical contingencies around them, but also feeding on what they have seen in the foreign press and books, or on what they have been told by European or Anglo photographers, critics or curators.

Revolution—whether it be a military coup or an authentic

JORGE MANUEL RILO (Argentina), Attacking the Government House, 1982

socio-economic change—characterizes Latino America in the Anglo conscience. While compelling and alluring, as were the social explosions in Mexico and Cuba, revolutions in the South are mostly viewed with fear. If not evil, Communist, revolution is strange, foreign. It is something dangerous and different, something alien to the values U.S. citizens live by.

The Pacific arena, in spite of China and Vietnam, is not percieved as revolutionary. It is not remembered as a hotbed of political intrigue. In the fissure between historical events and perceptual codes, Mao Tse-tung is far more overwhelming than Fidel Castro or Daniel Ortega, yet the revolutionary code is more consistently attached to the flesh of Mexico, Cuba or Nicaragua than to the body of China or Vietnam or North Korea. One could attribute this to our proximity, to the Western roots that were the legacy of Spain—fanatical beliefs, the "Le-

genda Negra" and the Inquisition. In contrast, an atmosphere of mystery and manners, of Confucian ceremony, family and order imposed its visual hegemony in the Pacific. Ho Chi-minh was Uncle Ho.

When the image of the Mexican Revolution began to be blurred by the economic promise of Brazil, Argentina and Mexico, the Cuban revolution came along and reestablished the significance of Southern rebellion. This, followed by regional debt and the Nicaraguan revolution, was set against the "orderly" economic growth of the Pacific rim, and consolidated our revolutionary image. The Mexican rifle and sombrero, Fidel Castro and his beard, Che Guevara and his beret, the Marine fatigues that metamorphosed into the rebel uniform of Latino America are branded in the consciousness of the rest of the world. The images carry a message against economic greed and the consumer society. But the economy-minded, conservative, narcissistic eighties have conspired to muffle the visual impact of the revolution in Nicaragua and other parts of Latin America.

Station 2: The Lover The Latin lover needs to be brought back into focus to understand its full genealogy. Its roots lie in the films of the twenties, followed by the stars of the forties and fifties, by César Romero and Carmen Miranda and by playboy Porfirio Rubirosa (who made it along with Kim Novak, Zsa Zsa Gabor, Barbara Hutton and others), and was kept alive by U.S. tourism "south of the border." The mythology of the Latin lover reached such proportions amongst the women of pre-sixties puritanical America, that *Esquire* ran an article before the

war, published anonymously as "Latins are Lousy Lovers":

"They are not only short; they are thin, too, with narrow shoulders and wide hips; in other words, like the Flapper-Age trousers—bell-bottomed. Their teeth—if any—are either frayed stumps or dazzling with gold. They wear straw Kellys too large or too small, badly fitting suits and shoes that pinch their feet—and they have little feet. Of course, they have nice eyes—that is, when they aren't cross-eyed. Their hair is oily and usually needs cutting. They spit a great deal. They are always scratching themselves."

Photographers in Mexico, Brazil, Venezuela or Cuba still take photos of passionate couples, of male dandies. Walker Evans, in his Cuban portfolio of the thirties, included several impecc-

PEDRO MEYER (Mexico), *Breakfast*, 1975

MARIA EUGENIA HAYA (Marucha) (Cuba), Esperanza and Chenard, 1981

RAUL CORRAL (CORRALES) (Cuba), Incoherence, 1982

ably dressed males. What is remarkable about the *Esquire* article is its portrayal of Cuba as the land of the prototypical Latin lover.

"This is the typical Cuban for you. That is what they're like if they look like Cubans. Most Cubans don't look like Cubans. They look like Germans, Italians, Swedes, Polacks, and clerks from Yonkers. It makes my heart bleed to think of the boatloads of hopeful females who go down there every year on cruises, trusting to find a nation of César Romeros."

Long before Barthes and semiotics, the Latin lover was a sign defined by *Esquire* in the paradox: "Most Cubans don't look like Cubans."

The South was the land of music, hot food and passion. The North was the land of hard work and puritanical constraint. The image of the Latin lover faded after the permissiveness of the sixties. But it still endures as a sign and can be seen in the ads of Georges Marciano.

Codes outlive their birthplaces and life spans. Lovers, the passion of a less affluent society and its instincts, are still subjects for photographers' eyes: passion in spite of age (as in the dancing couple by Marucha), and the crude beauty of primitive people (Roberto Fontana). Grounded into the lens of the Latino photographers is love, passion, instinct, nature.

Couples, as we reverse the coin, only become civilized by marriage. And marriage—which can become something extravagant and ludicrous—is also part of the sign. Marriage sanctifies instinct, and therefore must be coated with the artifice of culture.

Latino American photographers are quite different from their images. They are, as a rule, whiter than their work. By white I mean both the tint of their skin and the coloring of their mind, caught between the social awareness dominant in Latino American cultural life, and an awareness of Western technical and artistic critieria. The Latino American photographers usually belong to the bourgeosie, are Western-oriented and politically committed because of the pressure of the environment. If we were to photograph them, their clothes and surroundings would not belong to any of the categories recorded in their work: they look outside themselves to express a stand.

The possible exceptions to this are Argentinian photographers, who are more inwardly turned, focusing on psychology—neurosis or even madness—or on the quirks of their own class. The city is stronger than the pampa: they wish to assert their urban, non-Indian, non-rural image of themselves. They feel they are transplanted Europeans, such as Canadians and Yanks, in spite of their economic dependency and their history of military regimes. They would rather be peripheral Westerners than central Latino Americans.

In general, Latino photographers share a political content and a didactic intent. They share a moral focus, which, to a great extent, is conditioned by their existence outside of the market. They exist away from the mainstream of photojournalism, news coverage, advertising, coffee table books and annual reports. The fact is that most international newspapers and magazines get their photos from international news services and their ads from metropolitan centers. What is left is local news coverage, mostly limited to mug shots and political events, or sporadic corporate assignments. Because of this, Latino photographers are hungry animals. They work within a more elitist, cultural atmosphere that places value on exploring meaning and truth; they yearn for galleries or the possibility of success abroad—of being discovered in Europe or the United States. The internal market is limited. Support and subsistence income from the powers that be is moot compared to that of the painters and writers who live off the national budget. Only in 1978, with the "Hecho en Latinoamerica" photography colloquium

DANI YAKO (Argentina), Tango at the Congress, 1984

celebrated in Mexico, did photographers assume a regional presence.

There is a frontality in most of their photographs, a static, passive, composed world within the frame that is at best rigorous and at worst rigid. Most images seem to include the photographer, to lack any element of surprise—there is hardly a single "decisive moment." Most photos are therefore closer to Strand than to Frank. This goes to the heart of a basic Latino way of looking at the world. The world for us is more of a plaza than a mall. We live in a plaza. It is a space to gather, to see and be seen, to exchange gestures and words. It is not, as in the dominant Anglo approach to public places, a space to eat, skate or shop. Walk around any U.S. city where the Latino presence is strong and you can be sure that wherever you see a group gathered at a street corner, before a building or around a bench in the midst of Broadway traffic, they are speaking Spanish (if they are not black, for blacks also live in the plaza).

The space of the plaza is similarly dominant in Latino American photography, and means that you don't shoot obliquely, that you let yourself be seen, included, accepted. The photographer is part of the group, with a presence looked at, felt as an absence from the image.

Photographers like Roberto Fantozzi of Peru have chosen to work within a thematic consistency that is more textured and painterly than journalistic or sociological. Fantozzi's images show fabric, either alone or inhabited, but always worn, abused, wasted and still alive. They make a strong statement about what is lacking. These tattered people, these hanging cloths, talk to us about the missing abundance of clothes, of high fashion, of rivers of materials that are consumed and cast off before they achieve the wasted warmth of Fantozzi's images.

Station 3: Religion Religion takes two roads in Latino America: the oppressive weight of the Catholic cross and the instinctual liberation of African or aboriginal syncretic practices. Religion is not Protestant ethics but inquisitorial Catholic powers; it is not a Sunday social ritual but a daily appeal to Shamanism. This imagery of Latino American religious life and death appears as a force against enlightenment.

Religion in Latino America, independent of the signs that constantly interfere with visual discovery, has spun in the late seventies into a revolutionary force. Liberation theology, in spite of a conservative Polish pope, has grown to the extent that the Nicaraguan revolution could easily be labeled Marxist-Christian instead of Marxist-Leninist. This a station of the Via Crucis that will continue to grow.

Station 4: U.S. Penetration The socially minded photographers have included in their portfolios the presence of the United States through economic penetration. There is always the contrast between Coca-Cola and national identity, or Pepsi quenching the insatiable thirst for justice of the Amer-Indian.

Station 5: Nature In the films of Luis Buñuel, animals always stand for passion and instinct, blind to reason. The burro and the parrot, the street dog and the backyard fowl have enriched the photographic sign. Animals link Latino America to the earth and to a more primitive existence, decoded as either positive, as the myth of the natural; or negative, a sign of our under-development. If the car is an emblem of an urban society, the burro and the street dog are signs of the dominant rural society abundantly portrayed in Latino American photography.

Although urbanizaton is a growing fact of life in the region, it is not a decisive photographic theme. Urbanization is often seen as the new oppressive force acting on the peasants that crowd into the cities in search of employment. The urbanization of Brazil, Mexico, Venezuela or Colombia is either ignored or photographed with mistrust. The signs of rural life, although linked to underdevelopment, are often portrayed as positive statements of authenticity. There is always a conservative streak in art that looks at the past when it is endangered or about to disappear, and ours is no exception. *Cien años de soledad*, the novel by Gabriel García Márquez, looks more toward the past than at the present or the future. It is conservative in its effort to preserve. In a changing world these artists might be producing reactionary works as a desirable reality, a magical mystery. This ambiguity runs through most Latin American photography as well.

Station 6: Children A final category, the sign of the future in the Latino American via crucis: children. An overwhelming presence in Latino American photography, as well as in the demography of the region, children overflow into the streets,

MARIA EUGENIA HAYA (MARUCHA) (Cuba), The Photographer of Coyoacan, 1986

ROBERTO FANTOZZI (Peru), Lima, 1985

PEDRO MEYER (Mexico), Quasimodo, 1986

CAMILO LUZURIAGA (Ecuador), Untitled, undated

into the plaza. They are innocence and the future. They are not the fruits of marriage, but the fruits of the earth, of passion and concupiscence.

Children are a powerful sign because, in the midst of the agony, the changes in the region, they stand for an unknown future, a future that seems always endangered. Too young to work, they are still not in school or at home as the children of development would be. It is one of the most authentic, surprising and ambiguous testimonies of Latino American photography.

Understanding these six signs of the Latino American via crucis, the fault line that separates North and South, seems to make the contradictions more evident and sharper, as we seem to be turning in opposite directions along the axis of the continent. We belong all to the family of man (and woman) but we live differently. We conceive of social development along different roads, we make love under different impulses. Religion is relative in Anglo America, but in Latino America it is a search

for the absolute. Children grow up on both sides, but their futures are radically different.

We are fated to clash and/or coexist. If the original division between Anglo and Latino goes back to the XVI century, the present gulf is not between Spain and England. The South has not been able to develop economically in the wake of the transfer of technology and heavy investment; moreover, the Latinos seem to have an itch for radical socialism if left on their own. The situation might not be explosive, but the misunderstanding seems to grow. There is no longer a dream of continental integration and interdependency, only a limited expectation of coexistence.

I write this in the hope that we will not miss each other as we travel. We are doomed to inhabit the same hemisphere. We might understand the way the South makes noise and the North acts in silence, but the difference lies in how we harmonize our common humanity.

PEDRO MEYER (Mexico), The Annunciation of Graciela, 1980

PEDRO MEYER (Mexico), The Double Mask, 1980

Graciela Iturbide: Rites of Fertility

By Macario Matus

The ancient Zapotecans used to say that they were sons of beasts and ancient trees, born from the caves and the jungles, from the rivers and the sea. And for that reason, they always loved animals. So that when, at the foot of "tiger mountain," a village was born, it was called Tehuantepec; and when, among the flowers, another town arose, it was named Juchitan, which in Mexican means "the place of white flowers."

Thirty-five kilometers from the city of Oaxaca, in Yagul, the temple is dedicated to the frog, while in the ruins of Zaachila (the second most important Zapotecan ceremonial center), homage is paid to the turtle god, and in Macuilxachitc there are friezes representing the hunt of the alligator and the deer. In the sculptures, stelae, vessels and collections of jewels made by Zapotecans, zoomorphic forms are everywhere. In their legends and stories, as well, the protagonists are animals, while in the daily ceremonies animals appear and disappear.

Juchitan holds nighttime ceremonies called "velas," accompanied by much ritual dancing and drinking. In one of these ceremonies worshipping the alligator (vela guela bene), an alligator is suspended from a tent pole while below hundreds of men and women dance, drink, and eat, as an offering to the mythical beast. The dance of the tiger still flourishes in Tehuantepec, as do the dances of the monkey, the coconut, the leaf, and dances consecrated to the turtle and the fish. The life of the Zapotecans is still bound to the world of animals and flowers.

Among the range of folkloric songs and dances alive in the isthmus of Tehuantepec are those of the strand turtle (the Zandunga), and the weeping woman (the Medi Xiga). Each has its own history, reflecting the lives, habits, and mythical concepts of the Zapotecan race.

The story of the strand turtle concerns the life of a serious fisherman who hunts deep sea fish, shrimp, and turtles. The fish are caught with the help of an "atarraya," or casting net, the shrimp in a little trap. Depending on their sizes, the turtles are captured with different tools. It is a difficult job to "hunt" a turtle in the middle of the ocean, partly because turtles live in the depths, only going to the shore to spawn at certain times of the year, generally in spring and the months of November and December. Because of that problem, fishermen prefer to collect their eggs beneath the sand. If the eggs are not taken, the turtles hatch along the shore and then crawl to the sea. The fishermen know exactly which day to look for the turtle eggs and on that day take hundreds of them to sell in the markets of the Isthmus of Tehuantepec.

But this mundane activity of the men of the sea is transformed—as in so many folk rituals—into a sacred song, a dance: the ceremony of the strand turtle. It is performed at the culmination of the important ceremonies of the people of the isthmus—at weddings or other happy events. Most of the time, it

GRACIELA ITURBIDE, Sacred Hands, 1986

GRACIELA ITURBIDE, Girl with a Comb, 1980

GRACIELA ITURBIDE, Rosa, 1980

GRACIELA ITURBIDE, Magnolia with Sombrero, 1986

GRACIELA ITURBIDE, Serafina, 1986

is performed by a woman and a man. He wears his "charro 24" and she adorns herself with the typical apron of the isthmus. The style of their dance is like most of the ritual dances in Mexico: he circles around her seductively, while imitating the act of picking up turtle eggs and placing them in her skirt. The movements are repeated several times with special music, to create a theater of the act of love, of fertility, of the mating of the earth (man) and the sea (woman).

Another Tehuantepec ritual, the Red Fish, is a dance of unique significance. It is performed during the early hours of the morning, just after the deflowering of the bride by her bridegroom. The joyous mood of this ritual dance celebrates the happiness of the family, and honors the young girl who came to the altar a virgin. (In the house of the non-virgin bride, a perforated, hollow, battered pot is placed in the lintel of the door to indicate that there is no fiesta after the consummation of the marriage. On the other hand, girls who have "exorcised sexual passion from their bodies" will listen to the song of the Red Fish, as the guitars and the marimba strike up music in the night.)

The song of the Red Fish (the Huachinango) celebrates purity, virginity, honor. In the house of the groom, in the middle of the night, and after the consummation of the marriage, women relatives of the bride dress the girl. The bride then reclines on a bed covered in white sheets so that the guests can better admire the evidence of her virginity. The nuptial bed is covered with roses—red to announce that festivity of virginity, the deflowering; red color is poured on the white sheets as testimony to the amorous adventure of the night before. Surrounded by red bougainvilleas, red tulips, red roses, flowers chosen by relatives of her future husband, the bride waits.

Then the guests arrive, the women wearing headdresses of red flowers or iguanas, carrying bouquets of more red roses, the men bringing quantities of wine. The roses are woven into crowns worn by the bride's friends, who are there to witness that the young girl had been pure, pristine, chaste.

Once honor has been proven, the tune of the Red Fish is played, signifying the joy of the two families forever intertwined. Then the trumpets hurt the senses, speed up the feet and make the heart jump with joy. The music of the Huachinango carries in its words and notes strong and aggressive erotic allusions to the night just passed by the young couple, which the guests appreciate. The music moves the hearts of the guests, especially the bride's relatives, because they know now that their daughter, "everybody's daughter," "came out well," "salió buena," as the saying goes.

The women dance, bottles of wine in hand, and sing and joke about virginity and defloration, in a robust game of words and wild sensuality. The men do not dance at all, but their song is accompanied by a male voice that recites verses with double meanings and plentiful allusions to the deflowering. The voice sings of the sensuous shapes of fruits, and recounts stories of sexual behavior that would embarrass the lewdest pornographer. The Huachinango's original lyrics were written by Eustaquio Jiménez Jirón (a Zapotecan poet), but are now overlaid

GRACIELA ITURBIDE, The Ascension, 1985

GRACIELA ITURBIDE, La Senora Guadalupe, 1987

GRACIELA ITURBIDE, Magnolia, 1986

with the verses of other erotic poets. The performance, the lyrics, the dance of the Red Fish, is a spectacle equal to the most exotic traditions.

Where some remote part of the Far East joins the Zapotecan race, the origin of the "Medi Xiga" might be found. Just as the Zapotecan race had been a communal society from time immemorial, building sanctuaries, palaces, pyramids and houses, so their festivals are imbued with that same spirit. Today, the Zapotecans who live on the isthmus of Tehuantepec still hold their major ceremonies with communal feeling, called "Guela guetza," which means the union of physical strength and intelligence (for either good or ill: life or death).

Marriage is a major event of Zapotecan life, as is the construction of a Zapotecan house, and both bring together friends and relatives. Marriage in the isthmus can come about in two ways: by a man's asking for a woman's hand and by deflowering. The first ritual is generally preferred by the educated and the second is more common among the people. Both ways culminate in linking men's and women's hands.

Before the happy conclusion, a big festival is held, generally on Sunday beneath an arbor built with green palms, banana leaves, coconuts and a lot of white paper flowers. The young couple walks through the center of the arbor to receive the blessing of the godparents, who take their seats near the couple after placing two coins of silver or gold on their foreheads. The godparents carry with them baskets full of clay figurines representing fruit and domestic animals, to be shared with the guests, who are then supposed to give money to the couple. During the ceremony, the guests dance around the couple to music. In dancing the "Medi Xiga," the revelers attempt to break the clay objects of those nearest to them, and often end up in a lively battle in which all the ceramics are broken.

This ritual still holds powerful connotations, and together with the consummation ceremony in the weddings of the isthmus, acquired fantastic, barbarous, heavily romantic interpretations. In recent times, the ceremony has become a financial gift from the community to the young couple, called "Guendaliza," that is, a communal effort toward the happy beginning of a new life.

(Translated by Eniac Martinez and Nan Richardson.)

GRACIELA ITURBIDE, Hens, 1980

GRACIELA ITURBIDE, The Chickens, 1980

BEHUA SHIÑA

Behua xhiña canezu rini
tantu gudou bidua chita,
ma gudxhe li ora cuindini
nin la bidua ne nin la dxita.

Yanna bitopa zudi huinu
gui huini shi bira shou gueela,
pa nu balana nu guendaxheela,
ne pa la co, guza chubinu.

Ne zana guié ne zana guidxhi,
ma ca cului ni guca gazi,
na qui sutide ndi nabi dxhi
za xudxe tata cadi nazi.

La guya chahui de pe iratu
na pipi do, nahuini guichu,
nguen na xa xquipi, zaqueca xpichu.
xheela sha lia pa nga pe natu.

Yanna ma zanda ide nu rinni,
shi dxhi ti son, ica ti diana,
shi dxhi ti son Badu Xapa Huini,
tu que guya zucanu yaga.

Lague la xudxhi diti diti
la gata zaa ti pipi huini,
ni nu xaguete, mape naniche
sica ora xupi bicuhuini.

EUSTAQUIO JIMÉNEZ JIRÓN

(Written in Zapotecan)

THE RED FISH

Red fish, you're bleeding
From eating so many macho bananas,
When you get it up I've told you,
No banana, no eggs

Now lift your skirt
To see how you've livened up,
Wedding bells will ring if you're a virgin,
If not, come on, let's go home.

The flowers will know, the people will know,
What's been recently opened looks good.
This won't be a dry celebration,
I'll drink and everyone will drink with me.

Take a good look all you here,
So lovely, and covered with peach-fuzz,
Straight below the womb is her sex, too,
Husband and wife, and nobody doubts it.

Now let's drink the wine
Let's play a song, a diana*
Let's sing the song of the virgin girl
and whoever doesn't dance will have his punishment.

Drink deep, down to the bottom
Be happy with your whole body
For whoever is underneath, what pleasure!
Like a dog, lap it up.

EUSTAQUIO JIMÉNEZ JIRÓN

*(a cheerful song) Translated by Lisa Rosset and Nan Richardson

GRACIELA ITURBIDE (Mexico), Our Lady of the Iguanas, Juchitan, 1980

Sergio Larrain

By Agnes Sire

This is the shadow of the photographer, a man at the very least a dreamer as he cuts out, "rectangle in the hand," * these fragments of reality. We learn to see in his wake what we would not see without him, the magic moments that approximate the astonished gaze of a child—not a vision from an overbearing concern for information, nor from the efficiency of the image-hunter in action. What Sergio Larrain tells us, if we read into his narrative, has more to do with poetry, with a desire to make palpable a state of grace, a moment of intense perception, a moment of love, in which the click of the shutter gives birth to a fragile image of improbable destiny.

Valparaiso 1957: ethereal little girls suspended in the light of endless city stairwells, the hardness of a stone thrown—who knows where? These pictures, among others, indicate the ambiguity of a search for peace charged with latent violence, Larrain's constant concern. "Disquieting strangeness," anodyne and significant at the same time, Larrain's perception of the world challenges our own way of seeing. The question has less to do with the frame, "the decisive moment," "the absence of the photographer," than with the sudden eruption of a superintensified reality (previously invisible) which we recognize immediately as meaningful. A state of grace, certainly; photography, without a doubt.

* *El Rectangulo En La Mano* is the title of Larrain's first book.

The photographs which follow were taken in Chile with the exception of: pp. 29, 35, 37 top, Buenos Aires; p. 34 Bolivia.

LA HORA SEÑALADA

Está bien   el paraíso lo perdimos por precario
comodato de ángel guardián   éra la hora
desolojados fuimos a lanzazos   a besos
mejor dicho he armas   (no quiero herir a nadie)
Nos han vedado el cielo   ya el infierno
Es el limbo   estamos donde estábamos
nos cobijan aqui   es la verdad
pero eso es todo
Ahora que vagamos en busca de la luna
oscura está la gleba   los caminos
marchan sobre sí mismos   era la hora
La hora señalada se dispara en la sien
Sólo puertas mentales se nos abren ahora.

JUAN CAMERON

THE SIGNALLED HOUR

Fine   so we lost paradise because
of some guardian angel's broken lease   it was time
We were evicted at spear-point   nudged out
at gunpoint I mean   (I don't want to hurt anyone)
They've banned heaven   and hell too
It's limbo   we're right where we were
they give us shelter   it's true
but that's all it is
Now that we wander in search of the moon
the plowed earth is dark   the roads
walk down themselves   it was time
The signalled hour shoots itself in the head
Only the doors of the mind open for us now.

JUAN CAMERON

LOS DIAS DEL POETA

En los días de su vida
hubo acontecimientos tristes
y amables.
El cielo cambió de color muchas veces
y la lluvia del sur
-rencorosa-
lavó cada invierno
la tierra que él lamió en su infancia.

. . . pero el día de su muerte
fue un día oscuro y frío
rodeado de otras días oscuros y fríos.
Un país feamente agrietado se le aleja.
Qué vieron sus ojos pequeños y ávidos
por último vez:
toda la poesía sumida en un pozo,
o el fuego devorando ciudades,
o los hombres diluyéndose como sombras de sombras
mientras un río turbio precipita su cólera animal.
En los días de su vida hubo acontecimientos
tristes y amables,
ocurrieron muchas cosas hermosas
y otras
imposibles de comprender

OMAR LARA

THE POET'S DAYS

During the days of his life
sad things happened
as well as some pleasant things.
The sky changed color many times
and the angry rain
in the south
each winter washed
the earth that he put in his mouth as a child.

. . . but the day of his death
was a dark and cold day
surrounded by other dark and cold days.
A country covered with ugly cracks slips away from him.
What did his small, avid eyes see
toward the end?
all poetry sinking in a well,
or fire devouring cities,
or men dissolving like shadows of shadows
while a dirty river brings on his animal rage.
During the days of his life sad things
happened as well as some pleasant things,
many beautiful things
and others
impossible to understand.

OMAR LARA

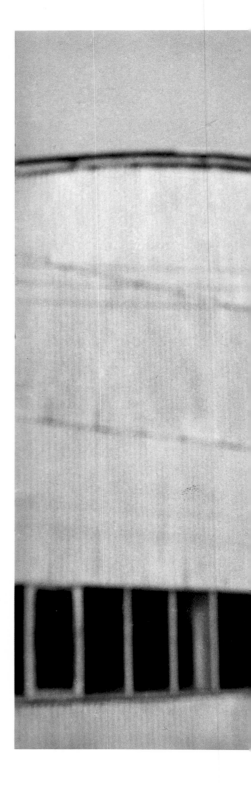

VI

Chile está lejano y es mentira
no es cierto que alguna vez nos hayamos prometido
son espejismos los campos
y sólo cenizas quedan de los sitios públicos
Pero aunque casi todo es mentira
sé que algún día Chile entero
se levantará sólo para verte
y aunque nada exista, mis ojos te verán

RAUL ZURITA

VI

Chile is far away and is a lie
it isn't true that we ever took our vows
the countryside is a mirage
and only ashes remain of the public places
Because even though almost everything is a lie
I know that someday all of Chile
will rise just to see you
and even if nothing exists, my eyes will see you.

RAUL ZURITA

Miguel Rio Branco: The Indians of the Future

By Eduardo Viveiros de Castro

They are neither people of the past, nor living fossils of a pre-Columbian paradise. The Indians of Brazil belong to a tumultuous present in their struggle to find a path amid forces and processes of planetary import. They are exemplary, for they face a problem shared by all of us, of creating a future which will not mean squalor and indifference. More than ever, theirs is the challenge of *becoming Indian*, of imposing the value of singularity against the non-value of abstract generality; for the elimination of difference is the destruction of the world, and the whole fabric of life may be resting, in a hidden and obscure way, upon the fact that there still are some Indians, somewhere.

The one hundred and eighty Brazilian Indian societies living largely in the Amazon River Basin have a total population of some 220,000. As a people, they are now confronted with new and massive threats—or with old ones which have gained impetus, attaining monstrous proportions. Mining companies, timber companies, agro-industrial enterprises, huge dams and hydro-electrical power plants, gold rushes, frontier expansion, highways, military invasion of their territories "to guard national borderlines," a state-entertained ideology of forced "integration" and "assimilation"—the enemies of the Indians are many and powerful, public and private, national and international. The encroachment upon their lands is encouraged by government policies of planned negligence and tacit recognition of the lesser right of the Indians to the earth they live on. Considered *de jure* as Brazilian citizens (albeit with the civil status of minors), they are *de facto* treated as conquered peoples, as war enemies of the state. They are seen as a nuisance by the government; as a shameful reminder that Brazil is not a "totally civilized" country; as obstacles to full-fledged capitalist expansion in the Amazon region.

In fact, it is a kind of miracle they have been able to survive—and even to grow in numbers—in the last decades. They evidence much more than a merely residual capacity to keep on living: their voice begins to be heard on a national scale, as they organize to fight in the political arena alongside allies who no longer content themselves with nostalgic evocations of the *bon sauvage* of Western imagination.

But the struggle is a difficult one: not only because their opponents wield power, but because their power forces the Indians to embrace the way of the enemy, to learn to use their weapons—law, political discourse, monetary economy—in order to resist them. The challenge, then, is how not to cease to be Indian; instead, how to become Indian through this very process, while taking from the white man the skills needed to live in a new (and worse) world. The Indian of the future will not be a hybrid of the "traditional" and "modern" cultures, but a transverse line connecting the particular and the universal in singular ways, a force of divergence which will potentialize difference to a new level of intensity.

The destiny of the Indians is our own destiny, for we all are the Indians of somebody else. It is not a question of race, or culture, not a question of essence; but a question of resistance, of movement, and finally, a question of beauty.
We should try to learn—to see—something with and through them: something as subtle as their subtle ways of dealing with the jungle; something as sophisticated as their talent to make a world out of so few people and objects; something that speaks of elegance, and joy, clear smiles in shining faces, laughs that betray a humanity we seem to have almost forgotten.

Rio de Janeiro, Brazil June, 1987

The photographs which follow, of the Gorotire Indians of the state
of Pará in northern Brazil were taken in 1983.

44

Sandra Eleta: Portobelo Unseen

By Nita M. Renfrew

Portobelo is not an idyllic place; great ports never are. And for over a century it was the greatest port in the New World. Never an ordinary coastal town, its energies were too long tied up with the fortunes and failures of the New World. A field force developed there over the centuries which was never lost, and still carries much of the same power. Portobelo was, is still, a place where peoples' dreams could be either broken or realized. It gave and it took, affecting the fortunes of the kings and queens of Europe.

Like all tropical places, Panama's Portobelo resists clear boundaries. Jungle and ruins and people all take turns encroaching upon each other; none of them is permanent. Any choice made is quickly eroded by the natural elements, and emotions here are raw and sprawling. Ideas with only short roots branch out rapidly; they grow up out of nowhere and then die back just as quickly. But when the liquid air gets so weighted down that it breaks into a thunderstorm, there comes a flash of lightning, a sudden, sharp focus, then another and another. The storm has lighted up.

When San Felipe de Portobelo was discovered and named by Christopher Columbus in 1502, it seemed, in the words of his son Ferdinand, "very large, beautiful and populous and has about it much cultivated land."

In 1595, when English corsair Sir Francis Drake destroyed Nombre de Dios, the port that till then served as main transit point for the precious goods being shipped from Peru to Spain, Philip II of Spain decided to move the town to the nearby bay of Portobelo. He commissioned Italian architect Juan Bautista Antonelli to design both the new city and the defense system to protect its harbor. Ironically, Portobelo was soon to become Drake's gravesite when, having died of dysentery, he was laid inside a lead coffin and sunk in the turbulent waters at the mouth of the bay, never to be recovered.

Antonelli designed Portobelo in strict adherence to the master plan set out by the *Laws of the Indies* for important maritime towns. The Spanish Empire and the Catholic Church both demanded majestic and lasting testimonials to their temporal and spiritual authority. Thus, from the outset, land and resources were allocated to this end, including two main streets leading to a central plaza, a town hall, a church, a prison, a hospital and the most important custom house and royal treasury of South America.

Warehouses, inns and gambling houses, as well as mansions belonging to rich merchants were built within town walls. Antonelli, famous for his military construction, also built the five main forts around the harbor and the many supporting fortresses and watchtowers. However, despite the magnificent defenses, the pirate Henry Morgan was able to conquer Portobelo less than a century later, extracting a heavy ransom from its governor before marching on to destroy Panama City.

The trade fairs held at Portobelo came to rival Seville in magnificence. Every year, the large open market was held for a month or two. But continuous assaults by pirates and foreign powers on Portobelo's coffers eventually made the defense of this trade center too costly for Spain. After the 1739 conquest of Portobelo by a British admiral, there were no more fairs. The great seaport was relegated to the status of a mere province, and the Spanish fleet took to rounding the southern tip of the Americas rather than risk shipping the goods over Panama. The road across the isthmus, from the coast of Portobelo to Panama City, had predated the Panama Canal by several hundred years as the key trade route connecting the Atlantic and Pacific Oceans. Through the sixteenth to the mid-eighteenth century this road was the way to get the treasures from Peru to the fleet that returned to Spain every March from the Caribbean—until the jungle took over. During the next two hundred years, Portobelo went into such a state of decline that it almost ceased to exist.

Then, in the nineteenth century, the California gold rush created a new need for a land bridge over Panama. However, the

SANDRA ELETA, Catalina, Queen of the Congos, 1980

SANDRA ELETA, Pajita, 1984

SANDRA ELETA (Panama) Fillio, 1984

SANDRA ELETA, Glory, Palm Sunday, 1972

SANDRA ELETA, Josefa, Healer of the Evil Eye, 1980

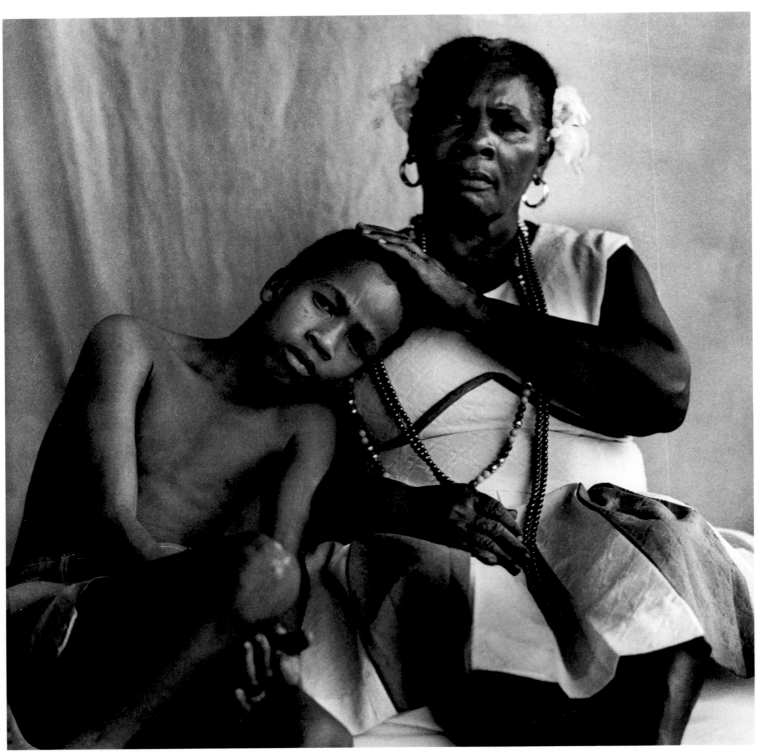

SANDRA ELETA, Ventura and Palanca, 1972

SANDRA ELETA, Congo Laganiza, 1983

miners came, not to Portobelo to start their journey over the isthmus, but to the nearby port of Colon. In 1850, the railroad was built. And eventually, the Panama Canal. Well into this century, although Portobelo was within short reach of an important crossroads of the commercial world, its existence was barely remembered and it was accessible only by water. Paved roads, electricity and telephones came very late to Portobelo.

Sandra Eleta was the first important ship to dock in Portobelo in a long time. When she went to the town in the early 1970s, it was to take possession of a two-room house left by an old plantation worker to her family. Portobelo was a dark shadowy creature, surrounded by bright liquid green forest, and waiting for prey after sleeping for close to two centuries.

The image of tranquillity, as in much of the tropical Third World, was only a mask to cover a certain kind of struggle for survival. No struggle for food in Portobelo—fish and fruit are plentiful. But rather, a struggle for focus, for definition: the necessary ingredients to enter the modern world.

There was never anything idyllic about Portobelo, except on the surface. Panamanians are quick to point out that the people of Portobelo are lazy, that they will not take ordinary jobs. But work in Portobelo was never that of an ordinary place. Its people lived by selling illusions with a heavy dose of reality, sometimes more of one, sometimes more of another. They dealt in possibilities, not in finished products. They were hustlers, as people in great ports have always been, living by their wits. When the Spaniards left, only the blacks stayed, descendants of the cimarrons, the runaway slaves, who also lived by their wits, the ones who were able to escape to freedom. At Carnival time, Portobelans still speak Spanish backwards, a ruse in the early days to keep from being understood by their masters.

For Sandra Eleta, living in Portobelo meant going back to the fundamentals of her childhood and away from the coldness she had found, the depersonalization favored by the intelligentsia of the world's capital cities. Portobelo was guts and richness and ferment—the stuff of soap opera—in the bowels of the Third World. And like a soap opera, a great seaport deals in cliches in their purest form. Sandra Eleta has recorded them—artificial and posed, like cliches always are, but no less real for this reason. Love, beauty, play, sickness, loss are all there in her work. The beauty of a cliche at its best is its immediacy, its ability to convey emotion without intellectual filters. In this way, Eleta bridges the reality of the Third World and the West; the Portobelans like them as much as Westerners do.

Despite the surface sophistication, the formality, the attention to esthetics, Eleta's photographs are rooted in popular Latin American tradition. The stories they tell have their origins in the melodramas portrayed in the *fotonovela*, a variation of the comic book, that uses photographs of actors to tell stories. Although there are no bubbles with words on the pictures, it is easy to imagine them. As Eleta says, "I search more for a dialogue than a capture of moments." Her pictures of Portobelo tell a story of fishermen and children, in sickness and at play, of woman as healer, warding off the evil eye, and woman as the once-a-year queen of Carnival.

The other place and time in which Portobelo existed whirled Sandra down into the hopes and needs of a people that had little in common with our description of the world. The inhabitants of Portobelo found a treasure in Sandra, but they fought over her reality just as she fought over theirs. Not knowing how to step into the world she brought to them, they almost destroyed her. To them she was the world of plenty, while theirs was a world of poverty. To her, it was the other way around.

Sandra brought with her the latest sound systems, fashion, bolts of colored cloth and shiny beads, paints and canvases, streamlined cookware, ideas for fishing and sewing cooperatives, and many people from other lands, some with money to spend. She opened up for them the world of consumer goods and travel—a world that had slowly disappeared when Portobelo had ceased to be a major crossroads. She was looking for a place to become, to be created. And Portobelo became her stage. Portobelo devoured Sandra, dismembered her and put her back together in ways that made her barely recognizable. Through her photographs, the amorphous shapes in her mind slowly became clear, took on sharp edges.

During Portobelo's days of maximum glory, it had been a magnet for profiteers and pirates and adventurers. And again today, through Sandra Eleta, it attracts wanderers from the far corners of the globe. She is Portobelo's main connection with the greater world. And in the invisible world that lives on, these blacks are still cimarrons, crafty enough to escape slavery and endure by their wits, who retain the identities taken on by their ancestors. They are still, under the surface, a people of the docks—sailors, stevedores, laundresses and cooks, blackguards, tarts and soldiers—selling their wares to a transient population. This is the hidden reality that the pictures of Sandra Eleta transmit.

SANDRA ELETA, The Congo Players, Moon and Sun, 1982

Photography in Latin America

by Maria Eugenia Haya (Marucha)

For a Latin American, the perception of his own image and reality through photography can only be a passionate observation. For plunder and suffering has formed the very substance of that image, forged out of extreme social contrasts and violent rebellion. Much in the confused life of Latin America has been bound up in that image, and our anger surfaces when we find, hidden in the beginnings of photography and buried by time, that all our glory has been spirited away.

Was photography born in Latin America? The Brazilian researcher Boris Kosloff demonstrated in 1976 that it was—as did Thomas Wedgewood, Niepce, Daguerre, Talbot and others in Europe. In Brazil, at the Villa Paulista de Campiñas, Hercules Florence improvised a laboratory between the bindweed and jicarasa, where by alchemy and witchcraft, Florence discovered through the processes of extraction and retention of the image the formula for light. Since the year 1833 (according to Boris Kossoy), Florence had been photographing with a camera oscura, using glass negatives and sensitized paper.

Florence published his discovery in the magazine *El Fénix* on October 26, 1839, when the daguerrotype had yet to appear in Brazil. But it was not until 1900 that the *Revista del Museo Paulista* published documents in Florence's family's possession, that proved his invention. Volume VII of the *Encyclopedia International*, published in 1920, printed the following citation under the title "Florence, Hercules,": "Credited with the discovery of polygraphy and photography (1832) in the works of Niepce, Daguerre, Talbot and Pitevín, of 1833, 1834 and 1850 . . . ."

Kossoy continued to investigate Florence's contribution to photography, verifying his findings scientifically at the highest level, and checking Florence's sensitization processes with Professor Thomas T. Hill of the Rochester Institute of Technology. He also carbon-tested fourteen of the Florence originals, to corroborate the following:
1) The attribution to Florence of the origins of the photographic processes of sensitizing and fixing, consisting of chemical preparations for contact printing with solar light utilizing urine as a fixing agent (with very satisfactory results); 2) The first recorded use, by Florence, of the word "photography."

These facts, along with the use of the glass negative, were important in light of Florence's isolation in the interior of San Pablo and his distance from the European scientific and cultural milieux.

Research in hand, Boris Kossoy announced that photography was born in Brazil, and that this had been purposefully silenced for a century and a half. Even today, in spite of decisive proof, French experts do not accept the existence of Florence's isolated genius. More than once, the scandal of the irreverent image of the man from Brazil urinating on the sacrosanct plates has silenced them.

The Introduction of the Daguerrotype in Latin America The daguerrotype, as it was baptized in Europe, was the result of a photographic process commercialized over the world, and appeared in Latin America fairly early. We know some of its probable dates of entry: in 1840 to Mexico, Venezuela, Argentina, Brazil, Uruguay, and Cuba; in 1842 to Peru and Colombia. By comparison, the first photo studios opened in New York in 1840, in London and Paris in 1841, and one year later in Berlin.

From its inception, "the photographic adventure," as the invention of Keith McElroy was called, sent daguerrotypists from France, England and the United States to our continent. With rare exceptions, they never established themselves long in the same country. One can trace the names of these early daguerrotypists in different countries through the years: Halsey in Cuba and Mexico, along with Hoit, Doistua, Custin and Vallete; and in Brazil and Uruguay, the same Abade Louis Compte. The Loomis brothers both worked in Cuba and Venezuela, and Hungarian Pal Rosti followed Humboldt's itinerary during the years 1857 and 1858 across Mexico, Cuba and Venezuela.

Recent information on the daguerrotype and other processes in these early years show their development was similar to the European and North American. Photography in Latin America had many uses since its birth. Employed by naturalists and scientists, it became an aid in drawing and engraving, with miniaturists even painting on photographic plates to give a more lifelike character to their images. But the first daguerrotypists concentrated mainly on the portrait, which at the time was marked by symmetric and formal composition recalling neoclassic painting. The portraitists installed their galleries, according to their preference, in hotels, on roofs, and in storefronts. Infrequently, they hired some "native" assistant, and when they did, these people had to learn the business "by sight."

The First Images of War It appears certain that the first images of war were captured by Roger Fenton in 1845. Fenton was paid to photograph the war in the Crimea, but was asked to make images that would not alarm the city people who followed the events from their parlors, and much less the families of the men fighting at the front. The subject matter of this photography aired in such amiable terms that it must have given the impression of a boy scout excursion rather than a war.(It is curious how early the problem of the interested manipulation of the photographic image presents itself.)

The holiday character of Fenton's photographs led European

CLAUDIA GORDILLO (Nicaragua), Rio San Juan, 1983

and American researchers to affirm—and they established this for the world—that the first photographic images demonstrating the true horror of war are those taken by Matthew Brady and his colleagues during the war of secession in the United States (1861-65). Nevertheless, we can corroborate that the first images charged with the drama of war were taken by a photographer in Latin America during the bloody occupation of Mexican territory by North American troops in 1847, only two years after Fenton's falsifying images, and fourteen years before Matthew Brady and his colleagues.

The Multiple Impression With the daguerrotype of the early years, and the diverse techniques that coexisted with it—ambrotypes, calotypes, talbotypes, ferrotypes, and galvanotypes— photographers struggled to perfect the definition of the image. They approximated this goal by using larger formats, which required more time and energy, and, of course, raised the cost.

So the method proposed by Desderi between 1852 and 1853, based on a smaller format, possible through the introduction of the glass negative crystal, the multiple impression and the use of albumen, produced a rapid echo in Latin America. The

cheapened costs these changes initiated offered access to photography to a greater number of people from different social strata. To be photographed started to become something relatively inexpensive. And that, together with the rapid proliferation of photographic workers "born" in Latin America, led to the appearance of large and luxurious studios.

By the 1860's, steady customers filled the securely established studio franchises (which nevertheless had to answer to foreign commercial firms). In addition, some sidewalk photographers created modest studios of their own. The proliferation of studios in the interiors of each country, with their simple homemade backdrops and decorative accessories, rudimentary, but at the same time authentic, favored an important change in the character of the photographic profession. It led to greater freedom, and in the calling cards from the 1860's and 1870's, not only the upper and middle classes of society are photographed, but also the poorest people: the indigenous tribes of different regions, the African slaves and the Chinese immigrants.

There is a Latin American iconography from those years that, in spite of having been made by foreigners—almost always Europeans that settled among us over a long period of time—still presents certain choices made by the photographer both in treatment and the interpretation of his subject. This becomes obvious when we compare it with the stereoscopes and postcards for sale at the time, enterprises tied to the apprenticeships that began early in the 1860s, and which, through the modern machinery of the "companies" were sold to ourselves, by ourselves. Those stereoscope and postcard images represent the earliest of many distorted interpretations on a large scale through which we suffered and were consumed. It is interesting to see how the image projected from the first "picturesque" albums like one from Brazil, which includes the famous "pintoresco de la Isla de Cuba," engravings copied from daguerrotypes, and the ad by Underwood and Underwood with its exuberant landscapes, exotic decorations, bananas and coconut palms, with their "typical" characters, were set up as "stock shots" which already (and until very recently) were shamefully accepted as real. Given the companies' production capabilities, the avalanche of these images became a kind of dark cloak over the genuine image we already were making of ourselves: an

RICHARD ARMAS (Venezuela), Comandante Ricardo Alfonzo, 1974

image that was totally legitimate, and recognizably different from the "other" vision in its seemingly plain workmanship, its gravity and absence of dramatic tone, in the freedom and simplicity of the subjects. It is visible in the photographs of Eugenio Courret and Maury in Peru; of Marc Ferrez, José Ferreira, Eugenio and Mauricio, Alberto Henschel in Brazil, Lessman and Próspero Rey in Venezuela; Benito Pannunzi in Argentina, Octaviano de la Mora in Mexico, Lara and Gómez, Julio Racine in Colombia, Spencer and José Maria Bravo in Chile, Mestre, Serrano, Maceo, Arias and Fernández in Cuba, and many others, who have since reinforced the connection between photographic vision and their own culture.

By the 1870s, Europe and North America already relied on numerous specialized journals and photographic societies that organized exhibitions, and on large companies which manufactured equipment, chemical products and photographic materials and handled reproductions of collectible photographs which brought massive sales.

All this information sooner or later arrived in Latin America during the time our modest photographic bulletins began to appear. Photography still had not appeared in the newspapers, but capitalist expansion, the constant development and simplification of the photographic process, the ease and growing cheapness of photographing, gave rise to photographers nourished by a steady stream of amateurs. Together, they created an image of the Latin landscape that was romantic, pictorial, and natural.

Toward the end of the century, a Cuban photographer, José Maria Mora, became one of three important figures in studio photography in New York. Mora worked with Napoleón Saroney, who became famous (among other reasons) because of Mora's talent. Mora showed a special flair in preparing original and imaginative sets that combined painted backdrops with objects on different planes to create a feeling of depth and realism unusual for the time. After Mora opened his own studio, photographs of women seen through imaginary doors, windows, or ovals of flowers began to appear all over America, and Mora joined Saroney and William Kurtz in the triumvirate of fame of New York portraitists. Nevertheless, Mora is ignored in the history of photography.

Photography as Social Witness At the start of the 1880s Latin America began to break away from the European pictorial stereotypes which defined photography as "Art." Themes which, under conservative academic scrutiny, were considered prosaic, took on new significance. For many, photography was too realistic: life was hard, and that was how Marc Ferrez recorded it in Brazil. Ferrez, who presaged the exceptional work of Lewis Hine, recounted the hard life of the miner, as well as the harsh working conditions on the coffee plantations and in the city.

Within photography classified as "social witness" are images that are irrefutable proofs of the atrocities of war, taken in Paraguay in 1866 by W. Bati, and those documenting (with-

HUGO CIFUENTES (Ecuador), The Couple of the Corner, 1986

RAUL CORRAL (CORRALES) (Cuba), The Dream, 1959

out any cosmetic editing) the death of President Moreno in Ecuador in 1875.

One of the most beautiful examples of Cuban photography, which we have baptized "country photography," recalls the nomadic and provincial character of "mambisa" life between 1868 and 1895. In 1886, in the barrios and villages of Ecuador, both the strongest and earliest Cuban examples of "social criticism" can be found in the horrible images of the Weylerian Introduction of 1896.

A few years later, in Mexico, the most memorable photograph of a social turning point in Latin America was made : the Mexican revolution of 1910, recorded by the Casasola brothers. This monumental work, while an admirably descriptive document, is also an example of the heights poetic vision can reach. Intimate emotion is expressed alongside marvelous and epic action. In its description of the "passions and absurdities of Latin America," it is, perhaps, the greatest poem ever made about the resistance of a village, and one of the high points of photography as a testimony and loving expression of personal values in Latin America.

The Vanguard The infinite number of avant-guard artistic movements and theories that have appeared since the end of World War I precipitated significant change in artistic criteria. Photography continued throughout, evolving, apart from more specific values, to become more "photographic," while Latin Americans received all the artistic waves of "isms": Cubism, Dadaism, Surrealism, Expressionism. Photography opened a new expressive arena to the more restless photographers, whose unusual paths innovated new formal and conceptual language, like Horacio Coppola in Argentina, who as a student of the German Bauhaus in 1928, was already doing photographic work of technical perfection in a definite surrealist orientation; Benedicto Duarte in Brazil, who produced elaborate mounted photos; or José Manuel Acosta in Havana, an important example of a avant-guard artist, revolutionary, and man of his time, who left behind a powerful body of work.

Critic Néstor García Candini notes the arrival of important photographers who came to live and work in Mexico in the 1920s, and the environment of interpretation that discussion of their work generated, as well as the link they established with muralists and artists in general, encouraging exploration of the specificity of photographic practice and its similarities and differences with the other arts. In this period the young Manuel Alvarez Bravo appeared, working first in Oaxaca, and later frequenting artistic circles, sharing long hours of discussion with Tina Modotti, whom he met in 1927. Don Manuel became the stanchion, the father, of modern Latin American photography, consolidating the medium's independence by securing his own creative reputation. Alvarez Bravo developed a universal photography within traditional Latin American photography, and his name is practically the only one to transcend our frontiers.

It is interesting to note for the record that in Latin America

LUIS BRITO (Venezuela), The Disinterred, undated

at that time there were, besides our beloved Manuel, excellent photographers. Martin Chambi of Peru, for instance, documented everything that occurred around him from 1905 to 1958 with exceptional technical skill, suppleness, and humanity. When he died in 1973, he left a legacy of 18,000 negatives, perhaps the largest preserved body of photographic work produced by a Latin American. Similarly, Fernando Paillet of Argentina, besides being a photographer, led an active cultural life as a musician and actor, and created an exceptional study of his native Santa Fe. Colombia's Jorge Obando and Cuba's Joaquín Blez are possibly the finest portrait photographers of the continent. Blez's magnificent studies of the Havana middle class between 1912 and 1960 have an exaggerated beauty, full of imagination and gusto. And there are others to add to this impressive list.

Press Photography Though by 1880 the printed photograph (half-tone) had appeared in the North American press, and, a

JORGE AGUIRRE (Argentina), Have a Coke, undated

few years later, photographic prints by different processes were already appearing in the Latin dailies, it was not until the beginning of the century that press photography became an area of specialization. The information agencies founded in the US and Europe provided the majority of the photographs we consumed in our magazines.

Many of our Latin American reporter photographers were as qualified as the better North Americans and Europeans of the time. Nevertheless, they were not known outside their national boundaries. On the rare occasion when the international agencies used the services of a local photographer, they omitted his name; but these same agencies and publications gave very different treatment to North American/European photographers.

CLAUDIA GORDILLO (Nicaragua), Plaza of the 19th of July, 1981

ISABEL HARDOY (Argentina), Mothers of the Plaza de Mayo, 1985

When the "Crash of '29" plunged the North American economy, among others, into crisis, the U.S. government had the idea of cancelling the subsidy given to the country's poor farmers, and the Farm Security Administration hired a group of important photographers to document the tragic consequences of that absurd law. As a result, the whole world knew the desperate plight of the North American farmers, and also came to know Dorothea Lange, Walker Evans, and Ben Shahn, among other photographers.

In Latin America, where the situation became even more critical, where the monopoly of large ranches caused greater and greater unemployment and homelessness, where hunger was really hunger and the wave of agitation was repressed by the "Good Neighbor" with blood and fire, Latin American photojournalists documented everything. They took pictures of Sandino in Nicaragua, of the uprisings in El Salvador with their 10,000 dead, of the students and union workers murdered in Guatemala, of the fall of Machado in Cuba. Nevertheless, the rest of the world did not know at the time that those wonderful images were taken by (among others) Guillermo Castro, Edmundo Clavijo and Leo Matiz in Colombia, and Molina, Pegudo, Domenech and Lezcano in Cuba . . . to mention only a few. Our images didn't seem to interest the North Americans and Europeans. In place of these images, a "representative photo" was released that was adapted to the "refined" sensibility of the foreigner. Among the news photographs viewed as the

PABLO LASANSKY (Argentina), Untitled, 1982

CLAUDIA GORDILLO (Nicaragua), Miskito Dance Festival, 1985

major photojournalistic work from those years were those included in the book by John Farber entitled "The Cuban Revolution of 1933"; the author, one Sam Shulman, an International Photo photographer.

It hardly bears repeating that each North American penetration into Latin America was more brutal, controlling and determining every aspect of national life, and, as the power of the press expanded in the 40s and the 50s, the media were excellent allies. Petr Tausk, the eminent Czechoslovakian scholar, considers this era, when magazines like *Modern Photography, Popular Photography, Camera* and others multiplied and diversified, with increasing circulation, an important moment in the evolution of modern photography. It was the decade when The Museum of Modern Art in New York opened its doors to photography, when Steichen organized his "Family of Man," and when more and more monographs of the great masters began to appear.

Of course, all these changes and developments involved only North American and European photography. We participated as spectators, dazzled by so much progress. One can't ignore the participatory role of the media, including visual magazines such as *Life, Look* and others. As part of the Cold War strategy of the United States to counter the growing prestige of the so-

cialist movement after World War II, the media responded to the superpower objective.

The image of Latin America, then, was systematically sweetened and elaborated by foreign photographers, some of whom came to be famous as experts on the problems of Latin America. If a connection between the United States and some Latin American country was desirable, *Life* would publish elegant pictures of Mondrian composition, beautifying, for example, the petroleum fields of Venezuela. If the big tourism corporations needed to promote Latin America, we would appear resplendent in color, gold and feathers (and just this one time, the Andes would be more beautiful and majestic than the Colorado Canyon). When our indignation reached the point where we kicked the car of the visiting North American vice president, we were portrayed as savage neighbors with whom "geographic bad luck" forced coexistence.

Within this manipulated panorama the true image of Latin America didn't fit. Our neighbors to the North were interested neither in the authenticity of our own features, nor in the value of images made from inside our culture. They preferred to avoid the critical vision of photographers like Nacho López in Mexico, and José Tabío in Cuba.

In this context of coercive interpretation, and lack of respect, at least two exceptional moments allowed us to determine our image. In 1957, a picture was circulated all over America which contradicted the Batistan rumor of the death of Fidel Castro. In the picture, taken by René Rodríquez, a fighter of the rebel army, Fidel appeared holding the territory of the Sierra Maestra. Later, in 1959, the magazine *O'Cruzeiro* published the amazing photo taken by Hernando López, a Cuban photographer, of the assault of the city of Fomento by the legendary Che Guevara. López, an intrepid character straight from a Hemingway novel, flaunted strict police surveillance to develop the precious rolls of film secretly in the little lab of Aladino Sánchez.

After the period of the fighting in the Sierra, cutting a wide swath during the era of revolutionary triumph in 1959, an avalanche of photographers from AP, UPI, and Magnum descended upon Cuba. Those times were a priceless fountain of raw material for the manufacture of news. And it was the photos of Bob Taber, Andrew St. George, Lee Lockwood, Marc Riboud, and Cartier-Bresson himself that illustrated every article

on Cuba published in the outside world, in spite of the fact that the most moving documents of all, with the simplicity and poetry of our early rustic photographs, were taken by the rebel soldiers who fought in the mountains. All this explains, in part, the silence of our photographers, and the absence in our photography of a Latin American iconographic system. Under these conditions, "made in the USA," the development of the Latin American media and diffusion of photography just collapsed, to use an expression by Lezama, "like a circus tent."

In 1976 the Consejo Mexicano de Fotografía was created, an institution which has played a most important role in the organization, validization and development of Latin American photography. This association, founded by photographers and critics, convoked the First and Second Colloquia of Latin American photography on a basis that was truly explosive: expounding nothing less than the recovery of our image under the vindication of our own values, and the affirmation of a multinational identity in Latin America. In other words, it began

RAUL CORRAL (CORRALES) (Cuba), The Wedding of the
Militiaman, 1961

FRANCISCO CIFUENTES, The Miracle, undated

to put into practice what had been for photographers just a theory of cultural decolonization.

Since the First Colloquium, Latin American photography has proved its existence and above all, its urgency. From that moment the so-called "centers of power" in photography have had to live with a phenomenon that can be considered parallel. But our efforts cannot be weighed on esthetic grounds and much less under ethnic criteria. With a strong sense of unity between us, Latin American photographers have evolved as a solid front. And so, over these years, we have won back, little by little, recognition and prestige.

Time-Life devoted ten pages to our Latin American exhibition in its yearbook, and recognizing it as something unusual, Venice 79 also welcomed the Latin American show, programming a symposium with the show. The Centre Georges Pompidou in Paris, the Museo Español de Arte Contemporáneo de Madrid, the Kunsthaus in Switzerland, the Arles Festival in France, and many more welcomed the Latin America photographic phenomenon. Also significant in the development of Latin American

photography were the efforts of the Casa de la Cultura of Ecuador, an institution that recently celebrated their first conference on Ecuadoran photography, and the Casa de las Americas of Cuba, whose prize in Latin American photography garnered considerable prestige. The Minister of Culture of Cuba first established an award for Cuban photography, then included it in the Bienal of Havana, one of the most important events in the plastic arts of the so-called third world. The Ateneo of Caracas, Venezuela, the Casa de la Cultura of São Paulo, Brazil, El Archivo de la Imagen y el Sonido, Brazil have joined other institutions in Colombia, Panama, Nicaragua in establishing a strong Latin presence in photography.

If Latin American has developed a sensibility and character rich in hue, it is most of all because it is a photography connected with a world and its people, and because it represents its soul.

(Translated by Jeanine El Gazi, Romanie Rout and Eniac Martinez; edited from a presentation given at the Third Latin American Photography Colloquium in Havana, Cuba in 1984).

People and Ideas

OTHER AMERICAS
A review by Naomi Rosenblum

Other Americas *by Sebastiao Salgado. Text by Alan Riding. Published by Pantheon Books, New York, 1987.*

Some years ago, a friend took me on an automobile trip from Arizona through northwestern Mexico. Mechanical irrigation had turned the arid plain into productive commercial vineyards and orange groves, except where native villages existed. There, women washed clothes in trickles of muddy water at the bottom of arroyos. At a seaside village we ate a picnic lunch seated on beached dories surrounded by fish stench and swarms of flies. Small, hungry-eyed children wandered toward us from squalid shacks thrown together from cast-off tin, and silently devoured our proffered sandwiches and chocolate.

At the time, I was irritated at finding myself in that impoverished place, without architectural, archeological, or historical interest (the lodestars that usually guided my travels). But I soon realized I had seen something far more significant than the art-historical sites I had come to expect from travel in Latin America (and elsewhere). I had been given a salutary, if brief, glimpse of "another America."

This vision of real life in the developing world came to mind recently in connection with *Other Americas,* a book of photographs by Sebastiao Salgado. A Brazilian who now lives in Paris, Salgado traveled through the uplands and interiors of Bolivia, Brazil, Ecuador, Guatemala, and Mexico in search of images that express the oneness of experience among the *campesinos* of Latin America. Recently issued in an English language publication (also published in 1986 in France as *Autres Ameriques,* and in

Spanish as *Otras Americas),* the book features a title intended for Westerners who think "America" refers to the United States, or recalls touristic experiences in picturesque vacation spots south of our border.

We in the United States are certainly aware that political and economic entities exist on the large landmasses called Central and South America (after all, Latin Americans come to the U.S. for jobs and loans). As tourists, we have witnessed local customs and viewed native artifacts that indicate that life in those parts is vastly different from ours.

But the photographs in *Other Americas* embrace the world that tourists and government officials avoid. These images, made in the hinterlands throughout the region, portray the poorest souls—people for whom life seems to consist only of work, faith, and death. The photographs are unrelievedly sombre; the dark tonalities, the mountainous and inaccessible physical environments swathed in mists, the close-ups of features and limbs from unaccustomed angles, all suggest an interplay of personal dignity and authentic sorrow in the face of inexplicable experiences. The profound bond between faith and work are summed up in an image of four men carrying timber in a mountainous area of Mexico. Wooden planks strapped horizontally to their backs form a cross and the procession through the mist brings to mind a modern Calvary. In another image, the figures of a man and a woman with a child bound to her back are gleaning in a burning field. Unlike the bucolic French painters such as Millet, who viewed peasants as heroic larger-than-life figures, Salgado sees these individuals as dwarfed and bowed within a vast landscape and darkly clouded sky. His sense that despite personal dignity and deep faith the misery endured by the poor of Latin America is

without solution is inherent in the final image of the book, in which an aged-looking woman and two children stand in a desolate hilly landscape before a gate fashioned from cruciform trees and crafted lumber. The male wage earner is absent—possibly off trying to earn a living—and the gate leads nowhere. It is a brooding and dispiriting summation of life on the land in Latin America.

In *Other Americas,* the decision to keep the pictures as large as possible within a visually attractive layout meant that most of the forty-eight images are printed across two pages, with the gutter slashing through in a disconcerting manner. Only a single line of type indicates the date and location where each photograph was taken. A three-page introduction by correspondent Alan Riding of *The New York Times* was probably meant to provide some historical and social context for what we see, but offers little explanation of the historical background or reasons for the poverty and desolation so apparent in the photographs. Additional text by Salgado reinforces the idea that layers of mystery, suffering, and nobility constitute the essence of life in these parts, but does not add significantly to the penetrating thrust of the imagery.

As an intense portrayal of physical and psychological realities, *Other Americas* undoubtedly will add fuel to the current argument about whether the role of documentary photography is to foster understanding or to elicit sympathy. In that light, this publication becomes an example of the documentary work they reject, because it moves the viewer to profound emotional empathy, but does not lead to greater comprehension of the factors that govern the social and cultural circumstances portrayed.

Herein, therefore, lies the conundrum: how to make sense of what we see and

Sebastiao Salgado, *Mexico*, 1980

feel? Those who maintain that the documentary style has outlived its usefulness would solve the problem by demanding that the camera elucidate reasons and connections. One strategy might be to include incontrovertible signs that are emotionally neutral within the images themselves. Another solution could be to add written texts to the images. Still another approach entails the use of sets of contrasting images, whose ironic juxtaposition would enhance knowledge.

Other writers and critics, myself included, hold that one of the valid roles of documentary style *is* to arouse feelings, that photographs need not function as politically and socially instructive tracts. Indeed, no images on their own are capable of explaining complicated political or social ideas. Nevertheless, the images in *Other Americas* do seem to cry out for explication.

One can envision a different kind of text, that satisfied the need for insight as well as empathy: text less involved with the "magic and mystery" that Riding favors than with an historical discussion of what has occurred in Latin America since its discovery by Westerners. I am not proposing a dull tract full of statistics, but a sensitive explanation by a Latin American aware not only of the religious and mythic urgencies of the culture, but also of the actualities of history and social

organization that have led to such hunger and poverty.

For example, Riding mentions the migrations of peasants from their native villages in the Guatemalan highlands to pick coffee, cotton, or to cut sugar cane in order for their families to live through the winter. It would have been helpful to learn that the commercial planting of huge acreages was forced on the region first by Europeans and later by North Americans. More interested in commercial gain than in the well-being of expendable small farmers, these outsiders, in collaboration with native landowners, consciously turned the fertile and varied agricultural systems that existed in the early eighteenth century into one-crop economies dependent upon imported food!

In another example, Riding refers to the Indians of Latin America (making no mention of Africans brought to the region as slaves, although Salgado's images in Brazil counter this omission) as powerless "losers" in the political battles fought by their compatriots of the right and the left. He leaves the reader with the notion that Latin American social and economic problems are insoluble and that its campesinos are pawns in political games. However, two centuries of rebellion and recent events in Cuba, Nicaragua, and other countries have shown that even

profoundly religious peoples will not endlessly endure misery, but plan and organize systems of redress, whether we in the United States agree with their solutions or not.

Because the images in *Other Americas* evoke a particular texture of life with such force, the lack of insight into the reasons for the intense religiosity and daunting poverty seems especially unfortunate. Without clarifying text, the book reinforces the notion of Latin American culture as exotic and incomprehensible, as not amenable to rational social solutions. This attitude may reflect Salgado's own nostalgia, after years of exile from Brazil, for the simplicity and directness of indigenous life. Certainly, his omission of all visual references to industrialization indicates that he believes that modern technology will not solve the problems of Latin America. Nevertheless, his chosen means of expression is a technological invention, and modernization, including camera culture, is an irreversible fact of life throughout Latin America. Indeed, the camera allowed Salgado, a former economist with the Brazilian Ministry of Finance, to find a compassionate voice. It enabled him to transcend the arid indifference of economic statistics and to force those who view the images to acknowledge situations they otherwise might ignore. Had these superb images been matched by a forceful and instructive text, readers might have been given an opportunity to understand the social and political realities to which the photographs refer—realities which have such important repercussions in our own political present.

RIO DE LUZ
Interviews by Esther Parada

During the last 3 years, 15 volumes of a major series of photographic books, known as *Río de Luz* (River of Light) have been published in Mexico City under the auspices of the Fondo de Cultura Económica . During the week of July 13–21, 1987, I interviewed several people involved in the creation of the series, and explored the origins and responses to this extraordinary publication effort. The following material, adapted from our conversations, remains as close as possible to the letter and spirit of the speakers.

Primarily, it seems to me that the books should be seen in the context of several traditions or currents of cultural activity in Mexico. The Mexican government has played an important role in the promotion and preservation of culture, especially through SEP (Secretaría de Educación Pública) and its dependencies such as INI (Instituto Nacional Indigenista) and INBA (Instituto Nacional de Bellas Artes); and through the publishing activities of the Fondo de Cultura Económica. This historic role is described in some detail by Victor Flores Olea, who is both a photographer and Undersecretary of Multilateral Affairs in Mexico's Ministry of Foreign Relations. He also serves on the editorial board of the *Río de Luz*, along with Manuel Alvarez Bravo, Graciela Iturbide, Pablo Ortiz Monasterio, Luis Cardoza y Aragón, Vicente Rojo, and Jaime García Terrés.

Excerpts from an interview with photographer Pedro Meyer, founding member of the Consejo Mexicano de Fotografia and international distributor for *Río de Luz*, trace the roots of the collection in the activities of the Consejo and the Latin American Photography Colloquia (the first two in Mexico City, 1978 and 1981; the third in Havana in 1984).

Photographer and designer Pablo Ortiz Monasterio, who serves as editor and coordinator of the collection, has had many years of publishing experience, first as coordinator of the Taller Editorial of UAM (Universidad Autónoma Metropolitana) in Mexico City, and then as editor of the *México Indígena* series published through INI (Instituto Nacional Indigenista). His own published books include *Los Pueblos del viento* and *Testigos y complices*. Below are excerpts from extended conversations with him, which touch on both the goals and problems involved in publishing the collection.

Photographer and editor Mariana Yampolsky has had many years of experience publishing art and educational books for the Secretaría de Educación Pública. Her comments shed light on these same issues.

It is a measure of the vitality of Mexican cultural life, and the importance and visibility of this series in Mexico, that

it is the focus of criticism as well as admiration by various members of the cultural community. Included here are challenges to the editorial policy of *Río de Luz* from two different sources: Raquel Tibol, cultural critic and author of numerous books on Mexican art, co-organizer of the first Latin American photography colloquium; and Eugenia Vargas, interviewed together with members of a group of artist-photographers I call "La Regla Rota" (The Broken Rule) because of their association with an iconoclastic contemporary Mexican arts magazine of that name. Both Eugenia and Armando are members of the Consejo Mexicano de Fotografia; Eugenia, along with other women, has formed a women's caucus within the Consejo.

In the final section Pablo Ortiz Monasterio responds to some of these critical comments and indicates future directions for *Río de Luz*.

This communication would not have been possible without the hospitality and generosity of many people in Mexico, especially Pablo Ortiz Monasterio and Marisa Gimenez Cacho, as well as the individuals quoted in this article. My gratitude to them and others whose observations enriched my understanding: Manuel Alvarez Bravo, Elena Poniatowska, Lourdes Grobet, Carla Rippey, Augustín Martinez Castro, Yolanda Andrade and Renata Van Hanffstengel.

VICTOR FLORES OLEA (from an interview by telephone, July 20, 1987):

There is a long tradition in Mexico of government promotion and sponsorship of political activity. This tradition was initiated basically after the Mexican Revolution, starting in the 1920s. We should keep in mind that it was the Mexican government that promoted mural painting in Mexico; the government turned over responsibility for murals in public offices directly to the important painters of Mexico and this contributed greatly to the development of mural painting—also of dance, music and other popular arts. It was through diverse state entities, such as the Instituto Nacional de Bellas Artes and the Instituto Nacional de Antropología that these activities were promoted. In other words, government took the responsibility of caring for the

national cultural and historical patrimony.

In the area of publications, the state also took a central role, especially through the founding of the Fondo de Cultura Económica. Actually the Fondo is an independent publishing agency, but linked to the government. It's what we in Mexico call a de-centralized state organism, which means it is run with public funds, with state supervision and oversight, but with full cultural and intellectual independence. Established in the mid-1930s, the Fondo published many of the most important books dealing with philosophy, political and economic theory, sociology, and history, including translations. This put these fundamental books into the hands of Spanish-speaking readers and scholars, making them available to Mexico, Latin America and Spain. So it was natural that the Fondo would be involved in the mid-80s in this *Río de Luz* publication series. . . .

It's not always easy for projects from Third World countries to make an immediate impact or achieve importance in the so-called First World—in the industrial centers or artistic centers. But in the measure in which this collection presents a coherent vision, Mexican and Latin American, an interest in social conditions and in the human condition of our continent, we think it will inevitably have some impact in other countries. It will make a mark not just because it represents documentation or witnesses a way of feeling, of living, but also because of its photographic quality and esthetic coherence.

Frankly, I think the developed countries have formulated a vision of much of the lives, the hopes, the political objectives, and the economic development of Third World countries which is distorted or incomplete, and frequently erroneous. I am speaking particularly of the United States' view of Latin America. In other words, the United States has not been able to recognize a fundamental fact: that the Latin American countries want to organize themselves according to their own traditions, their own historic and social characteristics.

PEDRO MEYER (from an interview at his studio, Coyoacan, Mexico, D.F., July 18, 1987):

This publishing project dates from when I was president of the Consejo [Mexicano de Fotografía]. We had proposed it originally to Bellas Artes so that they, together with the Fondo, could do something along these lines. For bureaucratic reasons, nothing came of this. But I realized that without this publishing project, everything we had accomplished through the Consejo and the Colloquia wouldn't have the intended impact. It was indispensable to have a publishing plan; and as long as we didn't have such a plan, we would always be constrained by the publishing whims or caprices of other places . . . with all that implies of dependence on market considerations, on their criteria for publication.

The opportunity came when Victor Flores Olea became vice minister of Culture [under the SEP: Secretaría de Educación Pública] when we began the Colloquia. He was the first to offer us support. Bellas Artes was under his direction at the time. It was minimal, but it was important to have this *official* support; with it as a base, we were in a position to seek further support. In 1978 I had raised money to publish the first Colloquium catalog, *Hecho en Latinoamérica I,* through the sale of commercial advertising (in the catalog). But just four weeks before it was due to come out, when the works from all over Latin America arrived, we realized for the first time the nature and scale of what we were dealing with; that it would have been totally incongruous to publish this with the sponsorship of corporations like IBM and Xerox. So I returned all the money and started to look for funding from other sources. Victor Flores Olea was very important in helping me to obtain funding from various government agencies, such as Petróleos Mexicanos.

When we were able to get this government funding and other support for *Río de Luz* I realized that we had advanced a great deal, but that without worldwide distribution our efforts were in vain. That final step—to make sure that the books reached the outside world, that they were commented on, talked and written about, circulated—is what we are addressing.

I don't think these books are destined for any kind of mass consumption. This isn't possible when the print run of each edition is not more than 3,000. This is an elitist cultural project: not because we want it that way, but because circumstances have made it that way. In the future it may be different. However, I think that in proportion to the numbers of books that are sold in Mexico, in relation to the population and to the [educational/cultural] level of the population, sales here are infinitely greater than the sales of similar photographic books in the U.S.. Let's say a book sells 1,000 in the U.S. and 1,000 in Mexico. That 1,000 in Mexico would be equivalent to 20,000 or maybe 10,000 in the U.S., considering the size and the economic level of the population. Consider that the U.S. has maybe half a million people studying photography, whereas here we have at most three thousand. So you can't compare numbers in any absolute sense . . . there are no equivalencies.

PABLO ORTIZ MONASTERIO (from interviews at his home and studio, Tlapan, Mexico City from July 13 to 21, 1987):

For me, the book is clearly the publication in which photography works best. True, in an original (photographic print) you can see all its qualities, . . . but when you have several images in a certain order, the logic of the book, it lasts a long time, . . . it's portable, it's democratic. In making books, I am using a very old form, but one that's influenced by something very modern: the visual language or narrative that has been developed through television and cinema. We are mixing that dinosaur tradition of wood, pulp, and paper with this modern language . . . . I am fascinated with this hybrid.

We are poor, but we make a special effort to do books, because we don't have a market to sell photographs and we can't organize a show that will circulate nationwide with lots of publicity. We don't have a lot of galleries or infra-structure, except in Mexico City. To circulate our discourses, the book is very important. True, our editions are small, but we don't have a market to do larger editions, to make the unit-cost lower. A lot of students are interested after seeing books in a bookstore or library, but not everyone collects them. Look, we have to start from somewhere. At first we did editions of 2,000; now we are doing 3,000. The economic situation is much more difficult now than seven or eight years ago, so people are not buying books, or not many, but even so we are making an effort. . . . Sometimes when I talk to you, you seem to be saying "Ah, these Mexicans are in Paradise, government agencies are investing in culture, and so on." But this is difficult, we have to spend a lot of time. It's complicated, it's expensive for the government too. Private publishers won't do it. . . . But we all understand in terms of political education, of how this nation is being influenced by other nations, that it is an important project, not for short-term, but long-term results, like your own FSA.

One could say it's a contradiction for such a poor country to have slick or precious books. But I think the quality of the printing, the resolution, the coated

paper, and other elements are important, precisely because of this. In a country like ours, the masses of people are basically illiterate and read poorly or little; but with media like TV we have learned to read the visual image. We could print more cheaply, with rough paper, not using duotones; but with duotones, and quality paper which takes the ink, well, we can read all the detail. In the Casasola book (*Jefes, héroes y caudillos*), you can see the faces of the women in the living room portraits or the decorations on the ceilings. Through those details people can see how the society lived during the Porfiriato, how rich they were, what style they had. You know, people learn from this. It's not only a matter of being slick for its own sake. Also, we are trying to get a market, not only ours, but also yours. The U.S. leftists might think our books are too slick, but we have to get your attention too, and if we just do little "pamphlets," nobody will notice. You are doing this interview now because we've made all these books and the collection got a prize at ICP [1986, International Center of Photography Honorable Mention for publications] in New York City last year, because the books are well done! Maybe you [North Americans] have reached a point where you have so many well-done books, where to do them roughly is kind of slick! You're around the corner already. We're still trying to convince people. I'm competing against boats and cars and Rolls Royce books that we import from the States . . . so it has to be presented in such a way that people are willing to see the poor people of Mexico City or other things that we photograph. Otherwise, it would become absolutely marginal. . . .

A roll of Tri-X is $4.00 in Mexico, compared to $2.20 in the States. There are no special prices, not even for professionals or people with special projects, and that is basically because of Kodak policies. They have two plants in Latin America: in Brazil they make paper and cameras, I believe, and here in Mexico they make film and chemicals. Everything is very expensive, but even when the Consejo asked for support for the Colloquium, we never got anything at all from them. The same goes for Polaroid, Agfa, Ilford, Fuji, and others. The people who received some materials got them

from corporations in Europe or the U.S., not from here, where the corporations are not interested at all. In general I would say that all of us in Latin America in the last ten years have gotten much poorer because of inflation. Everything—houses, material, cameras, to say nothing of going abroad or buying an imported book—these are possibilities that are almost unheard of now. I don't think that there are fewer photographers or fewer young people interested in photography, but we are all shooting a lot less, we are all printing a lot less, we are not making large prints, and we have to consider the economic factor every time we make a print or go out to shoot. For someone who has developed a way of working, this is not too critical. He can be more economical and not shoot all those frames that won't be printed anyway. But young people can't afford to be shooting all those exploratory rolls of film which are good for nothing, but which help them to become photographers. I think the long-range effects caused by the lack of experimentation now have yet to show.

I have a strong impression that black-and-white photography better suits our reality, which is painful and dramatic. Somehow, black and white is a more symbolic language than color. Color is closer to how we experience reality. So I guess we are attracted to the more symbolic black and white. . . . Also, I encourage people to do black and white because it's cheaper to reproduce, and as we have no market for selling photography as an object we are more into publishing. . . . People are doing color more and more, I guess because of the influence of the States. In that case, to do black and white becomes a kind of cultural resistance, which I encourage. But we cannot be close-minded about that. That's why we spent so much money on the Rio Branco book, because it shows a different way of using color, different from the mainstream of what they're doing in North America.

Somehow we have to produce the little grain of sand toward cultural resistance, given the influences which are so overwhelming in our countries—especially for Mexico, so close to the U.S.. The issue is not just color photography, but it's part of a whole package, with certain kinds of images, certain kinds of composition,

the whole way of working, which may have a rationale in the U.S., may respond to certain impulses there; but our reality is different. For instance, now the Mexican government (especially through the SEP) is pushing the Day of the Dead, because it got to the point where suddenly Halloween was all over the place and there were these plastic pumpkins and kids. . .dressed as witches, and the like. This is a tradition which has no basis for us, but through TV we picked it up from the States. . . . On the other hand, the Day of the Dead is part of a long rich tradition; it defines us as a community, as Mexicans. . . .

But cultural resistance exists at another level too, as, for example, in the publishing efforts of Francisco Toledo and the Ayuntamiento Popular (municipal government of Juchitán). They are spending a lot of money because their fight is not only against the big centers of power, of Europe and North America, but also against the central power of Mexico! So they are doing their own books, their own shows. The Lacandones are doing the same thing in Chiapas, in the jungle; and the Huicholes in a different way in Nayarit in the northwest. These people know that their political strength comes from their ethnic origin, so they keep it, they use it to negotiate. They have strong and rich traditions in their fiestas, their rituals, their incredible costumes. So a lot of people want to film them, to photograph them. They let people do it, but they charge for it. Not every time: they let you do it when you make friends, when they know it's to their advantage. But when a French TV team comes, for instance, they negotiate payment . . . it's not because they are afraid of the camera. . . . We might not agree in many things, but there is a nationwide agreement in terms of nationalism. . . .

Author of *Yo, El Ciudadano* (*I, The Citizen*) Nacho López was a photojournalist, working for magazines, the first Mexican to do photoessays. Many of his photos had already been published in the 1950s or early 60s in *Ciudad de México*, a cultural magazine. Fernando Bénitez, who is very well known as an essayist, and has written a lot about anthropology, did the text. He and López had worked together on several projects. Though you might not think all the pictures are great, to me *Yo, El Ciudadano* has the fascination of the city and goes beyond the eye of the photographer in its theme. Its sections were grouped into daytime, religion, and night life. The organization, which follows the subject matter of the material, and the use of bleeds, give rhythm to the book. Though I edited this book with Nacho, I didn't "sign" it (as editor). Later, starting with the book on Renau, I did sign the books. After the López project, the production changed: we went to a whiter paper and changed from copy camera to scanner for making duotones. We decided on one typeface because we definitely wanted the collection to look like a series. We didn't want it to be as rigid as the Italian Masters of Photography series; we wanted to achieve slight differences, by combining various colored inks with silver, for example, for the covers.

In *Dulce sudor amargo* (*Sweet Bitter Sweat*) Flores Olea had seen Miguel Rio Branco's work in Paris, so he proposed it for the series. Obviously the book is the best, in one way: it's very important, very Latin American. When Río Branco came he had it all together. He had worked with many people in Paris doing the editing. He had a different idea of the book—he wanted to have a different size. So for the first time I decided to have a different format (horizontal instead of vertical). The production was very expensive; but it was worthwhile. It is a book I find very interesting, unique, as important as *The Americans*. It's a breakthrough—remaining within the tradition of Latin American photography, but incorporating new elements in

its use of color. Rio Branco is a painter and makes movies too, you know, with a very personal point of view. Stirring. There is a strong sensation of flesh, of sexuality. I don't think he's with the lower classes, working for the revolution, but somehow he enters into certain universes and shows you, like Baudelaire, the terrible things about life. It's beautiful and it's painful—and somehow Latin America is like that.

Jefes, héroes y caudillos (*Leaders, Heroes, and Caudillos*) has been the best-selling of the series. Obviously this is not an objective history; there are many different ways of constructing the reality of this period. What I did was a very concise, brief view of the revolution, structured in terms of caudillos or personalities. I researched the vaults of the Archivo Casasola [The photo archive of the Mexican Revolution, administered since 1976 by the Instituto Nacional de Antropología e Historia]. I am very proud of this book, especially the section "La Decena Tragica" (the ten days when Madero was overthrown and killed and Huerta, the "bad guy" of the revolution, appeared) which is almost unknown material. I found this material in a box, a collection by Teixidor—a man from the 1940s who collected all sorts of graphic material, not just photographs, but also notebooks. He ordered and made some kind of sense of things, which is what we have to do. One of the things that I realized is that photographs of the revolution's dead are rarely shown, yet more than a million people died in the struggle. They (at the Casasola Archive) said, "Oh, no, [to show] this is sensationalism." I

said "No. It's the truth." We have to let it be known that there was a lot of killing. I didn't retouch anything, but I edited some of the images, cropped them . . . by cropping I give more emphasis.

In structuring the book I always tried to have a human side to the heroes, to show them with wife and kids, not just the great part of myth, but more familiar. This was difficult with Porfirio Díaz; he never allowed casual photos. The quality of reproduction here is so important; you can see detail in the face. Detail is eloquent; it speaks of time. This is why I insist on quality; there is a reason to spend so much time and energy and money. For example, I love this picture (from the Porfiriato, the presidency of dictator Porfirio Díaz), it reminds me of Lartigue. . . . Then Madero: showing the sister of Madero gives a familiar touch, humanizes him . . . he is not just a myth: you see his shoes dirty, the papers, the kid working. . . . Though they are still official photos, they construct a different image of Madero. . . .

You know the story of *Josep Renau: Fotomontador* (*Josep Renau, Photomontagist*)? We met in Cuba, with Fontcuberta [the Spanish photographer and historian who wrote the introductory essay]. I had heard about Renau in *Photovision*, but in our generation almost nobody knew about his photomontage work. He was a Spanish refugee who worked in Mexico with Siqueiros. He had been coordinator of propaganda during the war in Spain and organized the removal of paintings from the Prado to Switzerland, as they were going to be bombed. He commissioned "Guernica"! *The American Way of Life*

SUEÑOS
DE PAPEL

GRACIELA ITURBIDE
PRESENTACIÓN DE VERÓNICA VOLKOW

LOS
ENCUENTROS

VÍCTOR FLORES OLEA
PRESENTACIÓN DE CARLOS FUENTES

ESCRIBIR
CON LUZ

HÉCTOR GARCÍA
PRESENTACIÓN DE JUAN DE LA CABADA

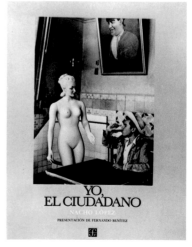

YO,
EL CIUDÁDANO

NACHO LÓPEZ
PRESENTACIÓN DE FERNANDO BENÍTEZ

was Renau's title for the collages done primarily in the 1950s during the McCarthy period. I signed this book "selection and editing by Pablo Ortiz Monasterio" because I selected and rearranged the images from Renau's book. For instance, I linked two (one of Cuba from the 1960s, one from Chile in the 1970s) by putting them on facing pages. I knew that I was doing something kind of daring in adapting Renau's version. I wanted to take responsibility for that, not attribute it to the Fondo de Cultura. I have reasons and can defend my position. I am convinced that we did justice to Renau, but I didn't just want to reproduce his earlier book. As editor, I think you have the opportunity of saying something about a body of work.

MARIANA YAMPOLSKY (from an interview at her home in Tlapan, Mexico, D.F., July 16, 1987):

Río de Luz is a series that's of great importance for photographers and for the country because even though we are moving in an economic crisis that is very severe, the fact that space is finally given to photographers as documentarians or as artists, speaks for the publishing house as taking a step in the right direction. We are not thinking of something that will immediately sell, but we are giving space to something that has been ignored up to now. It is a pioneer effort to create such a series; against all odds there are now 15 books! Mexico and other countries in the Third World have not considered the role of photography per se as being relevant. So this series will perhaps bring changes in attitude. As in any other place in the world now, photography,

much more so than any other communication art, is daily food. But people take it for granted. The photograph has always been a throwaway object! Certainly with an important series of books which stress the different nuances with different ways of seeing things, this will slowly be corrected. At least we hope so. . . .

If this series has a negative side to it, I'd say that perhaps it hasn't lived long enough. I would like to see other works by younger photographers; I'd like to see more varied works; I'd like to see other points of view. [On the other hand] I think there's a great deal of resentment among the photographers that is at a verbal level. But when you ask to see their work, you find there isn't that much. It's easy to say "Publish the young photographers," but there aren't that many with substantial work when you get down to the nitty-gritty. I think that's why Pablo opened the series to Latin America. And then the photographers themselves do not give the appropriate importance to their work. It's pre-selected before the editors see it; and it just might be that other things they've done have more importance that what they show. . . . Pablo is the first photo editor we've had in Mexico, or perhaps the two of us are. Other editors work in commercial magazines, and perhaps I'm ignoring them, though not maliciously. I think that Pablo is growing, and if the series goes on, or there is a new series, he will certainly be one of the people you go to feeling that you're going to get a fair deal.

THE "REGLA ROTA GROUP": ARMANDO CRISTETO, EUGENIA VARGAS DANIELS, ADOLFO PATIÑO, (from an interview in the home

of Adolfo Patiño and Carla Rippey, Mexico City, D.F., July 16, 1987):

VARGAS DANIELS: I love the *Río de Luz* collection, even though I don't find all the books equally good; but what is very obvious to me is that there are only two women published in the fourteen books. I don't know if this means they consider women photographers' work less important, or if they simply are not thinking about it. I think there are many women with interesting work, young women—for example, Lourdes Grobet, Lourdes Almeida, Flor Garduño. One wouldn't necessarily publish a monograph of each one, but a collective volume. . . .
PATIÑO: I think these books are too conservative. There's not enough attention given to experimental activity; and there's a lot of it in Mexico. It wouldn't have to be a monograph, but [there should be] a book dedicated to a group of people who have been centered around Jalapa and Veracruz. Also work in mimeography, work derived from Xerox or other photocopiers by people such as Santiago Rebelledo, Gabriel Macotela, Yanis Pecanis and Augustín Martinez Castro (who has experimented the most with color Xerox) and people who have worked with photography outside of a laboratory, in Polaroid for example, which would include such people as Jan Hendrix, Lourdes Almeida and myself. . . . There's no (published) evidence that these new things are happening in Mexico, parallel to what's happening in Europe and the U.S.. The Mexican state, the government in all its institutions, including the Fondo de Cultura Económica, which is a branch of the government, is

like an analyst with a psychiatric patient: he listens so the patient can let off steam. But do you know what the medicine, the treatment is—an aspirin, a palliative, a single page in a book, such as *Historia natural de las cosas;* this is the spoonful of sedative offered to us to smooth the cough. . . .

CRISTETO: *Río de Luz* represents a conservatism, a certain complacency, perhaps a single class perspective. . . . Why not publish Crabaneto? Why put two great photographers in one volume [Arias and Corrales are in *Cuba: Dos Épocas,* the newest title] when each of them has so much material? Why publish work as weak as that of Raphael Doniz and not accept work as rich and varied as Lourdes Grobet? Another problem is that the editors are imposing their own structure on this material. Many times the photographer is not in agreement, but in order to have his work published, goes along with it. . . .

PATIÑO: The book by Rio Branco is about the beauty of misery in Brazil. . . the beatification of misery. It's the same thing Pedro Meyer does in Mexico—the estheticization of human misfortune. Instead of spending these millions of pesos in publishing this book, I would prefer a magazine, with fewer pages, but more continuity, more variety. . . Sometimes I think that a series such as *Biografías de Poder* [Biographies of Power, an openly "revisionist" history of the Mexican Revolution in eight volumes, recently published in Mexico, using anonymous photographers] is a richer graphic history of our country, our traditions, than *Río de Luz.* . . .

RAQUEL TIBOL (from an interview by telephone, July 19, 1987): [In the series] there are so many images of campesinos but the vision of campesino life is anachronistic for Mexico. It is from the 1930s, what I would call Cardenista (from the presidency of Lázaro Cárdenas 1934-40) or indigenismo populista, (idealizing the native). It indicates an attitude of pity or compassion toward the poor. There are other kinds of campesinos, not necessarily the poor—what about documenting them? What about, for instance, jornaleros (day-workers) on the big agricultural estates of the North?

Or what about the Guatemalan refugees? What is missing in the series is a tougher vision—backbone.

There should be greater rigor in selection. Now there is too much repetition. For instance, there are too many images of angels, or religious pageants with angels. I don't want to see one more little wing! . . . In spite of all these problems, it is an exceptional collection.

PABLO ORTIZ MONASTERIO responds: One could say that these painters are very rigid (or narrow) in their use of images. Painting here in Mexico is related to the marketplace. It is very expressive of the individual, but doesn't have too much to say as social commentary. Or maybe their language is just too sophisticated and is not as easy to read. Listen, I encourage experimental work—I do it myself—but I don't believe in publishing work only because it is experimental, or because it is by women, or belongs to some category. However, Jésus Sánchez Uribe or Anibal Angulo or Gerardo Suter each have worked a long time experimentally, and I have asked them to present projects. Also, there are other places where artists' books can be published. I love little books, too, and have made my own editions, with rough paper and Xerox. Felípe Ehrenberg has done a lot with this kind of publishing. . . . But this material isn't appropriate for these "stuffy" *Río de Luz* books—just as Aperture doesn't publish a certain kind of alternative book. So there are different channels for different materials. Not everything has to be like *Río de Luz,* but this happens to be the style we presented to the Fondo. . . . About the [single] class perspective, I don't think it applies here. Even if *Río de Luz* were more experimental, it wouldn't represent a *different* class view. Experimental work also has a class perspective; it's also bourgeois, and you know, sometimes it's even more so—in the individual's personal preoccupation with his or her own fantasies.

However, I think the *Río de Luz* should grow with a greater emphasis on thematic books rather than on monographs and not just record "little angels" or other beautiful images. In the near future, we will be publishing an oversized book on the work of Manuel Alvarez

Bravo including a great deal of unedited material. The next book will be *Paso a la democracia [Transition to Democracy],* very interesting work by Argentinian press photographers from 1979 to 1985, with a text by Miguel Bonaso, an Argentinian novelist exiled in Mexico. Following this is a monograph on Hugo Cifuentes, an Ecuadorean photographer, and, lastly, *Mexican Daguerrotypes and Feurrotypes: 1840–1860* by Olivie De Broise and Rosa Casanova, art critics and historians. These books are just the beginning for us in Latin America to use photography as a more complex tool to talk about our reality.

The books published in the Río de Luz *collection to date are:*

Yo, El Cuidadano *by Nacho López; Introduction by Fernando Benitez, 1984*

Los Encuentros *by Victor Flores Olea; Introduction by Carlos Fuentes, 1984*

La Ráiz y El Camino *by Mariana Yampolsky; Introduction by Elena Poniatowska, 1985*

Sueños de Papel *by Graciela Iturbide; Introduction by Veronica Volkow, 1985*

Dulce Sudor Amargo *by Miguel Río Branco; Text by Jean-Pierre Nouhaud, 1985*

Escribir Con Luz *by Héctor Garcia; Introduction by Juan de la Cabada, 1985*

Historia Natural de Las Cosas: 50 Fotógrafos; *Text by Alvaro Mutis, 1985*

Josep Renau, Fotomontador; *Introduction by Joan Fontcuberta, 1986*

Jefes, Héroes y Caudillos: Archivo Casasola; *Text by Flora Lara Klahr, 1986*

Espejo de Espinas *by Pedro Meyer; Introduction by Carlos Monsiva's, 1986*

Retornos a Oapan *by Abbas; Text by Abbas, 1986*

Casa Santa *by Rafael Doniz; Introduction by Antonio Alatorre, 1986*

Luces y Tiempos *by Lázaro Blanco; Introduction by Guillermo Samperio, 1987*

Cuba: Dos Épocas *by Constantino Arias and Raúl Corrales; Text by María E. Haya (Marucha), 1987*

Andando el Tiempo *by José Luis Neyra; Text by Jaime Moreno, 1987*

CONTRIBUTORS

JUAN CAMERON, 1982 winner of the prestigious Gabriela Mistral poetry prize, lives in Valparaiso, Chile. His most famous book, *Perro de Circo* (*Circus Dog*) describing the human condition after the military coup, won the Rudyard Kipling Prize in 1978.

EDMUNDO DESNOES is a Cuban writer whose acclaimed novel, *Memories of Underdevelopment* (NAL, 1967) was succeeded by a book on photography and visual imagery *Para Verte Mejor* (*The Better to See You*) in 1979 (Mexico City: Siglo XXI). He is currently living and working in New York City.

SANDRA ELETA of Panama studied photography with Carlos Montafor and then at the ICP in New York. She is associated with the Archive agency and her first book, *Portobelo*, was published in 1985 by La Azotea (Buenos Aires).

MARIA EUGENIA HAYA (MARU-CHA) is a Cuban photographer, film director and historian living in Havana who is currently working on a history of Latin American photography.

GRACIELA ITURBIDE of Mexico photographs the spirit-life of the Indian peoples. She began taking pictures in 1972 and first visited Juchitan in 1981. Her photographs of Juchitan will be published, along with a text by Elena Poniatowska, in a forthcoming book by Ediciones Toledo (Mexico City).

OMAR LARA, founder of the Chilean literary magazine *Trilce*, chaired the National Meeting of Younger Poets of 1965, a dramatic cultural turning point which abruptly ended in 1973, when Lara, like so many of his contemporaries, left Chile for exile. A recent recipient of a Guggenheim Fellowship, Lara has returned to Chile.

SERGIO LORRAIN, a Chilean photographer, was a member of Magnum Photos until 1974, when he stopped taking pictures. A major retrospective book of his work will be published next year in France, Mexico and the United States.

MACARIO MATUS is a Mexican poet and writer of Zapotecan origin, and editor of *Guachachi Reza* quarterly (Zapotecan for "The Cracked Iguana").

ENIAC MARTINEZ is a young Mexican photographer working in New York who lived for several years in Havana while his father served as Mexico's Ambassador to Cuba.

ESTHER PARADA is a photographer whose work has been exhibited at Museum of Modern Art, New York, the Hirshhorn in Washington, D.C., and the Museum of Fine Art, Houston. She teaches at the University of Illinois at Chicago, and her articles on Cuba, Nicaragua, and media representation in Central America have been widely published.

NITA RENFREW, formerly of *Le Monde Diplomatique*, is a freelance writer for *Foreign Policy*, *Rolling Stone* and other periodicals.

MIGUEL RIO BRANCO lives between Rio de Janeiro and Bahia, Brazil. A correspondent with Magnum Photos, Rio Branco began his career as a painter, and has won numerous awards in both cinematography and photography. His book *Dulce Sudor Amargo* (*Sweet Sour Sweat*) was published by Rio de Luz (Mexico City) in 1986.

NAOMI ROSENBLUM teaches history at Parsons School of Design in New York. She is co-author of *The History of American Art* and author of *A World History of Photography* (Abbeville, 1984).

AGNES SIRE is Director of Special Projects of Magnum Photos, Paris and the editor of Sergio Lorrain's forthcoming monograph.

EDUARDO VIVEIROS DE CASTRO is a Brazilian anthropologist whose work with the Gorotire Indians has been ongoing for more than a decade.

RAUL ZURITA is a eminent Chilean critic and poet whose experiments with technique, mysticism and structure place him in the vanguard of the writing community in South America.

CREDITS

Pp. 16–26, from "Danzas Rituales y de la Fertilidad," an unpublished manuscript by Macario Matus, by permission of the author; pp. 28–38, poetry by Omar Lara, Juan Cameron and Raul Zurita from *Poets of Chile*, copyright 1986 by Steven F. White and the individual poets. Reprinted by permission of Unicorn Press, Greensboro, North Carolina; pp. 41–47, photographs by Miguel Rio Branco courtesy of the artist and Magnum Photos Inc.; pp. 58–69, edited from "fotografia en latinoamerica," a transcript of an audiovisual presentation given at the Third Colloquium of Latin American Photography in Havana, Cuba, in 1984, by permission of the author. All other texts and photographs are by permission of their respective authors and the artists.

ANDRE KERTESZ
Diary of Light 1912–1985

Foreword by Cornell Capa, Director, International Center of Photography, New York
Essay by Hal Hinson

The definitive book on the Hungarian master, in a limited deluxe edition of only 3000 copies, with 152 tri-tone plates, is published in conjection with the major retrospective exhibition this fall at the International Center of Photography in New York. It features a uniquely comprehensive essay by Hal Hinson, Kertesz's personal biographer.

208pp., 11 × 14, 152 black and white photographs;
Cloth $95.00, until January 31, 1988. $125.00 thereafter.
ISBN 89831-256-0

APERTURE TRAVELING EXHIBITIONS
CURRENT SCHEDULE

Mothers and Daughters
The Field Museum
Chicago, Illinois
January 15–March 20, 1988

Art Museum of South Texas
Corpus Christi, Texas
April 8–June 26, 1988

Boise Gallery of Art
Boise, Idaho
July–August 1988

New York State Museum
Albany, New York
December 1988–February 1989

Delaware Art Museum
Wilmington, Delaware
March–April 1989

Sioux City Art Center
Sioux City, Iowa
September–October 1989

Sheldon Memorial Art Gallery
Lincoln, Nebraska
January 9–March 1990

Contemporary Latin American Photographers
Southern California Contemporary
Art Galleries of the Los Angeles
Art Association
Los Angeles, California
September 27–October 28, 1987

Nan Goldin: **The Ballad of Sexual Dependency**
Media Center, Rice University
Houston Fotofest
March 1988

Robert Glenn Ketchum:
**The Hudson River and
the Highlands**
Mid-Hudson Arts & Science
Center
Poughkeepsie, New York
September 11–October 16, 1987

Paul Strand: **The Range of
Expression: 1914–1976**
Port Washington Public Library
Port Washington, New York
Summer 1988

Other exhibits
David Graham: **American Beauty**
Mitch Epstein: **In Pursuit of India**
Raymond Depardon: **Photographs
and Films**
Ralph Gibson: **Tropism**

**BURDEN GALLERY
SCHEDULE**
Paul Strand: **Maine Photographs**
September 22–October 31, 1987
Ethan Hoffman: **Butoh: Dance of
the Dark Soul**
November 3–November 28, 1987
Mitch Epstein: **In Pursuit of India**
December 3, 1987–
January 14, 1988

Aperture's traveling exhibition program circulates original Burden Gallery and Paul Strand Archive exhibitions.
To receive brochures highlighting current and future exhibitions,
contact Sam Samore, Exhibitions Director, Aperture, 20 East 23rd Street, New York, New York, 10010, (212) 475-8790.

**APERTURE/BURDEN GALLERY/PAUL STRAND ARCHIVE/PHOTOGRAVURE WORKSHOP
20 EAST 23 STREET, NEW YORK, NEW YORK (212) 505-5555**

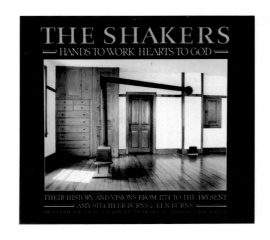

THE SHAKERS

HANDS TO WORK, HEARTS TO GOD

By Amy Stechler Burns and Ken Burns

Preface by Eldress Bertha Lindsay

Photographs by Ken Burns, Langdon Clay and Jerome Liebling, with historical Shaker photographs.

The most beautiful and radiant book available on the Shakers and the first to examine the true heritage and the extraordinary life and history of America's oldest spiritual community. By the prize-winning authors of the acclaimed PBS film, richly illustrated by noted photographers and texts from a variety of commentators, from Thomas Jefferson to Eldress Bertha Lindsay of the Shakers.

128pp., 11 × 10, 45 black and white photographs, 104 color; Cloth $40.00; ISBN 0-89831-267-6

Aperture takes great pleasure in presenting the new, redesigned, MASTERS SERIES, devoted to the works of the world's great photographers.

Remarkable in their exceptional quality and value, the elegant small volumes are available in paperback or hardcover at a wonderful low price. Texts and biographies by recognized critics and scholars like Mark Haworth-Booth, A.D. Coleman, Richard Pare, and Christopher Cox provide incisive and informative portraits of the photographers and perceptive commentaries on their works. Each book features elegant duotone reproductions and the entire MASTERS SERIES is produced with the same high standards of quality that all Aperture books are celebrated for.

Collect one, collect them all—THE MASTERS SERIES make wonderful gifts!

PAUL STRAND, HENRI CARTIER-BRESSON, MANUEL ALVAREZ BRAVO, ROGER FENTON, AND DOROTHEA LANGE, AND COMING SOON: EDWARD WESTON!

96pp., 8 × 8, 40 black and white photographs: cloth $14.95, paper $9.95

ORDERING INFORMATION Please write or telephone your order to Aperture, 20 East 23 Street, New York, N.Y. 10010/(212) 505-5555. Include your name, address, and daytime phone number. Send a check/money order, or indicate your Mastercard or Visa number (with expiration date) and the titles you would like to receive. Add $2.00 per title for shipping and handling. New York state residents should add sales tax. Standing orders for the entire set of THE MASTERS SERIES are accepted. If you would like to know more about Aperture's publishing program, please write or call for a current catalog.